WOMEN COLOR
DAILY DEVOTIONAL

The New Women of Color Daily Devotional SUMMER

The articles and prayers are taken from the *Women of Color Devotional Bible* © World Bible / Nia Publishing Co.

Urban Spirit! Publishing and Media Company is an African American owned company based in Atlanta, GA. You can find more information at http://www.urbanspirit.biz/

The New Women of Color Daily Devotional Summer Edition © Urban Spirit! Publishing and Media Company

Special thanks to:
Stephanie Perry Moore, General Editor
Dr. Charrita D. Quimby, Content Editor
Brionna Jones, Editorial Assistance
Produced in assistance with Cheryl Wilson
Design and Production, Larry Taylor, LTD2

Choice Books: 979-8-9853690-2-1
Urban Spirit: 979-8-9853690-1-4

Manufactured in the United States of America

WOMEN of COLOR
DAILY DEVOTIONAL

JUNE - JULY - AUGUST

urban spirit!
inspire higher

TABLE OF
CONTENTS

Month	Week	Theme	Contributor	Page
June	1	Self-Care	Jackie Graves Butts	7
June	2	Creativity	Dr. Charrita Danley Quimby	22
June	3	Father	Orbra H. Porter	43
June	4	Fellowship	Gwendolyn A. Mason	62
July	5	Wisdom	Sheryl Givens	83
July	6	Exploration	Jane Fox Long	103
July	7	Patience	First Lady Wayneshia Harris Perrymond	122
July	8	Integrity	Michele Clark Jenkins	137
August	9	Doer	Tia McCollors	157
August	10	Perseverance	Dr. Lakeba Hibbler Williams	176
August	11	Thriving	Dr. Rindia Lambert Hunt	197
August	12	Armor	Kymberlee Norsworthy	215
August	13	Holy Spirit	First Lady Jamell Meeks	234

DEAR SISTER,

Summertime is the perfect season to not only relax and vacation, but to also free your mind and focus on the love of Jesus. Thirteen fabulous women from all over the country have written devotionals (devos) that address important themes.

The goal of this book is for you to dive daily into the devos and allow them to be the catalyst to help you grow even closer to God. Each devo has a title, a thought-provoking question, a scripture, a short story, an application, and a closing prayer. When placed together into a daily devotional, the combination is a tool to help you dig deeper into the word.

It is our hope that the words on each page minister to your soul. May your journey in the months of June through August bring you peace, hope, and faith and the realization that no matter what month you're in, the Lord is always there.

God bless,

Stephanie Perry Moore
General Editor

JUNE
WEEK 1

DAY 1

RELAXING
MY WAY

Am I selfish?

"For we are his workmanship, created in Christ Jesus unto good works, which God hath before ordained that we should walk in them."

(EPHESIANS 2:10)

STORY

When Grace called her husband to let him know that she would not be home in time for dinner, she was not expecting an attitude from him. Grace had a long stressful day at work, and she was stopping to get a massage. He knew how stressed she had been lately. How could he not be okay with her decision?

After having an anxiety attack that landed her in the hospital some months back, Grace had

9

asked God for better health. With an understanding that she must prepare for her prayers to be answered, Grace made a decision to commit to taking time for herself to relax and de-stress. She would make her health a priority in her life.

Why could her husband not get this? Why did he always have to see her actions as selfish when they were actually selfless? Grace's thought was that her desire to take better care of herself would make her a better wife for him. If this was truly God's will for her, she needed help working it all out.

APPLICATION

In life, we get so busy taking care of others that we sometimes forget to take care of ourselves. There are many ways we can show love to God, but one of the most important ways is to love ourselves as God loves us. The Bible tells us that we are God's temple and that God's Spirit dwells in us. There are blessings that come with taking care of yourself. God wants us to be the best that we can be. Loving ourselves gives us the depth we need to love others.

Being selfish is defined as lacking consideration for others and being concerned only with one's own personal profit and pleasure. Selfishness is often viewed negatively. However, being selfless, concerned more with the needs and wishes of others than one's own, can also take a negative toll on your well-being and can keep you from being the best that you can be for others.

When you feel that you are overwhelmed with life's challenges and storms, know that you can trust God to know exactly what you need to survive. Take time for yourself and pray. God loves us and wants us to take care of ourselves first. We should look to Him for our strength and know that He will always be there for us.

PRAYER

Lord God, look down on me with eyes of mercy. Your favor covers me as my shield, and I know that You and only You can anoint me with the self-care that I need to conquer life's storms. Grace me with patience and wisdom that allows me to take care of others and myself around me. Help me, Lord, to create boundaries that will guide my selfless ways. In Jesus' name, Amen.

DAY 2
A HEALTHY SPIRIT

How do I really feel?

*"Know ye not that ye are the temple of God,
and that the Spirit of God dwelleth in you?"*
(I CORINTHIANS 3:16)

STORY

Grace had just finished volunteering at a homeless shelter with a couple of her sorority sisters when she got a call from her younger brother. She and Rod were so close growing up and had an excellent relationship throughout college. After college, Rod became connected to the wrong crowd and began using drugs. Grace knew Rod was trying to become clean, but she just could not keep financing him

while trying to take care of her own family. Just last month alone, Grace had given Rod $1,000, and she had lost count of all of the other money she had given him.

Grace had begun to get behind on her own bills, and her husband had taken notice. She answered the call from her brother, and sure enough, Rod needed money again. It took everything out of her to say "no" to her little brother, but Grace had to start somewhere. She felt awful after saying "no." Was this what God wanted from her? Did God want her to give what she did not have? Had her brother taken advantage of her for too long? Grace needed God's will to take hold of her fast because her spirit was all over the place after saying "no."

APPLICATION

God loves a cheerful giver, but so often, we give to a point that it hurts us. It is so important to take care of yourself first. Allow God to bless you so that you can be a blessing to others. The Bible tells us that every man shall give as he is able, not what he does not have. Giving without a grudging heart allows for a healthy spirit. When you give what you do not have, it creates resentment. Give generously, but understand that giving what you do not have to give will cause stress to your soul and will not contribute to a healthy you.

PRAYER

Father God in heaven, I thank You for my giving heart. Please forgive me for not understanding boundaries associated with giving. I ask that You continue to allow me to give generously, but at the same time, protect me from hurting myself in the process. Lord, You are better to me than I am to myself. I pray, Lord, that You continue to guide me and clean my spirit for a healthier me. In Jesus' name, Amen.

DAY 3

PEACE IN PRAYER

Where do I find peace?

"And he withdrew himself into the wilderness, and prayed."
(LUKE 5:16)

STORY

Grace hung up the phone in tears. How could she have not noticed the change in her appetite and the twelve pounds she lost in just three weeks? Her doctor had just shared the bad news with her; Grace's breast cancer had come back. How would she tell her husband and kids? She battled the ugly "c" word three years ago and won, but why was it back now? Things were going so great. Her husband had just landed a new job. Her oldest daughter was graduating from college. Her youngest son was a junior in high school and already captain of the varsity basketball team. Why now, Lord?

Grace could not even think of herself at this time; her thoughts were all about those who loved her. She needed some time for herself to sort this out. She decided that she would not tell her family right away. Grace would take a weekend trip alone to sort through her thoughts. She hoped her husband would understand. Grace needed time alone with God to share her feelings and to ask Him to help her beat cancer again.

APPLICATION

Often in life, issues and circumstances come our way that we cannot handle alone. We need God to help us get through. He tells us not to fear and that He will restore our health. God hears us through our prayers. Sometimes, it is important to take time to just pray to God and give Him all the glory. This might mean finding your own wilderness to isolate yourself and pray. Your wilderness might be a weekend trip to the mountains alone or maybe just solitude time in your own home. Whatever it might be use that time alone for prayer with the Lord. Prayer is self-care.

PRAYER

Dear Lord, my Father which is in heaven, with You I know that all things are possible. I pray that You will comfort me in my suffering, lend skill to the hands of my healers, and bless the means used for my cure. Give me such confidence in the power of Your grace that even when I am afraid, I may put my whole trust in You. In Jesus' name, Amen.

DAY 4
INCORPORATE "ME" TIME

Does anybody care about me?

*"And he said unto them, Come ye yourselves apart
into a desert place, and rest a while: for there were
many coming and going, and they had no leisure
so much as to eat."*

(MARK 6:31)

STORY

Grace was feeling good about herself on this particular Sunday. She had worshipped the Lord in a wonderful church service that morning. Heading home for a nice relaxing Sunday brunch with her family, she received a call from her sister Jade asking her to take their ill mother to the grocery store. Why couldn't Jade take her? The responsibility of their aging mother always fell on her. Grace's mom could not drive due to a stroke she suffered a few years back. Since then, it seemed that her siblings always put the burden of her transportation on Grace.

Grace was feeling overwhelmed. She had a very demanding career, her own health issues, and her own family responsibilities. Because she was the most responsible one of her siblings and always did things for others, they thought that she had all the time in the world to help their mother. Do they not understand that she has a life and that they should help their mother too? Grace wanted to do the right thing. She loved her mother, but she did not want to support her alone. What would Jesus do in a situation like this?

APPLICATION

At some point in life, our parents will begin to age. Some might even lose their ability to take care of themselves. When this happens, adult children often take on the caregiver role. In this role, we often get so busy taking care of others' health that we forget to take care of our own. It is important to be mentally healthy as well as physically healthy. God tells us to be anxious for nothing. Often, we might take care of our bodies but not our minds. We will visit an internal medicine doctor before we will a psychiatrist. We pray and ask God for a healthy body, not a sound mind. God promises us that He will strengthen us. Let us always make sure to give Him our troubles.

PRAYER

Dear Lord, the constant struggles and demands in my life feel intense some days. I feel weary and worn at times because of all of the demands that come my way. Thank You for being my refuge and my strength. Help me to trust You more and to stop burdening myself with people and things that do not bring me peace. Fill me with Your spiritual wisdom and discernment to do what is right for others and me. In Jesus' name, Amen.

HANDLING LIFE'S STORMS

Is it over yet?

*"God is in the midst of her;
she shall not be moved:
God shall help her, and that right early."*

(PSALM 46:5)

STORY

Grace was awakened from her sleep by the loud buzzing of her cell phone. Who could be calling her this time of the morning? It was 4:00 a.m. Grace answered the call and was told that her Aunt Maye had just passed away. This was the fourth death of a close family member in just a month for Grace. Why was God punishing her? First, it was her dad, then her first cousin on her mom's side, then her best friend from college, and now her favorite Aunt Maye. This was just too much!

Grace had always been the strong one in her family. As a result, when anything negative happened, she was always the first one everybody called. They had every right to call Grace because she really was the levelheaded one that always had answers. However, these close deaths had really taken a toll on her mentally and physically. She was being challenged like no other time in her life. Grace often found herself asking God, "Why me?"

The pain was beginning to become unbearable. This just might be too much for her to handle. How could Grace gather her strength and move past this? How could God make her pain go away or at least make it bearable? Grace needed help.

APPLICATION

Death is so final. It is one of those storms that never seems to end. Yes, it might calm here and there, but losing someone we love will always leave a void in our hearts. It is so important to ask for God's guidance when mourning the death of a loved one. Jesus told us that if we believe in Him, we will live and never die. We must remember this when dealing with the death of those that we loved. They really are in a better place because they believed. God tells us that we live and die for the Him. Believing this to be true will give us comfort.

PRAYER

Today Father, as I grieve for the loss of my loved ones, I find comfort in the fact that You also grieve for them. Thank You, Lord, for opening my ears to Your words, my eyes to Your truths, and my heart to Your message. The pain I feel is so deep, but I know that this too shall pass and that Your comfort will make it less painful for me in time. Take my grief and my exhaustion. Take it and renew me. In Jesus' name, Amen.

JUNE
WEEK 2

DAY 1
RECOGNIZING YOUR CREATIVE GIFTS

Have you discovered what makes you unique?

"And he hath filled him with the spirit of God, in wisdom, in understanding, and in knowledge, and in all manner of workmanship."
(EXODUS 35:31)

STORY

Carol's first real job after high school was as an administrative assistant to the CEO of a local nonprofit organization that developed programs to assist economically disadvantaged individuals within the community. Carol found her work to be interesting and exciting. The CEO, Charles, found Carol to be smart, eager,

hard-working, and committed. As a result, after a short time, he gave her additional responsibilities that allowed her to offer ideas about programs that would benefit the individuals the organization served.

In her new role, Carol learned a lot about herself. She learned that she was passionate about helping others and that she had many creative ideas. Not only did she have ideas, but she also developed strategies for implementing and accomplishing her ideas. Charles told Carol that she possessed a God-given gift to do this kind of work. She had never considered being able to do a particular job as a gift. She asked God to reveal her gifts to her.

APPLICATION

The scripture reference to "all manner of workmanship" refers to the many creative gifts with which God, the Creator, has equipped His people. Some have a narrow view of God's gifts, limiting them to only spiritual gifts, such as prophecy, healing, teaching and those specifically related to ministry. Others think of God's creative gifts as only artistic, as it relates to music, visual art, and dance. We should not limit our view of God's gifts. Creative gifts take many forms. In every area of life, God has gifted His people with the creativity to accomplish necessary tasks. God has gifted His people in the areas of leadership, athleticism, service, mentorship, research and discovery, business, finance, administration, counseling, writing, engineering, design, craftsmanship, hospitality, etc. The list goes on indefinitely. God's creative gifts are broad and widespread, not narrow and limited. Moreover, He often blesses us with many.

Now that you know the creative gifts of God cover every area of life, take some time to identify your own gifts. What is it that you enjoy doing? What do you feel drawn to strongly? What is it that comes easily to you? What is it about you that others often compliment? What is it that others seek you out to accomplish? What is it about yourself that makes you feel special? Your answers to these questions will help you identify your gifts. Be open-minded, recognizing that you cannot put God nor His gifts in a box. Just because what you identify as your gift is not commonly recognized as a gift, does not mean that it is not YOUR creative gift!

PRAYER

God, I ask that You reveal to me all of the creative gifts that You bestowed upon me and how I might use them for the furtherance of Your Kingdom. Open my mind, Lord, so that I do not place limits on You nor limits on my gifts. I thank You for trusting me with these gifts, and pray that You will be pleased with how I use them. It is my desire to glorify You with my gifts as exemplification of my thankfulness. I thank You for the wisdom, understanding, and knowledge that comes with these gifts. As these gifts within me are revealed, I pledge to remain humble and not boast. I will give You all of the glory, for without You, God, I am nothing. Amen.

DAY 2

DEVELOPING YOUR CREATIVE GIFTS

Have you nurtured and used the gifts given to you?

"Neglect not the gift that is in thee, which was given thee by prophecy, with the laying on of the hands of the presbytery."

(I TIMOTHY 4:14)

STORY

After seeing her creative ideas develop into programs that changed people's lives, Carol began to give more thought to Charles' statement about her "gift." If this was her gift, she wanted to use it to the greatest extent possible, but she wanted a greater understanding of exactly what she was doing. Did it have a name? She also wanted to make sure she learned everything she could about administering programs and leading a nonprofit organization. She went to the only person she knew had the answers, Charles. Having seen something special in Carol from the very beginning, Charles eagerly took her under his wing.

As her mentor, Charles exposed Carol to the ins and outs of the organization. He taught her about fundraising, finances, personnel management, grant writing, public relations, and politics. He allowed her to sit in on meetings, and she accompanied him on work-related travel. She was exposed to the full gamut of what it takes to lead an organization and influence change. Carol was a sponge, soaking up everything, asking lots of questions. The more she learned, the more passionate she became. God revealed to her that administration was her creative gift.

APPLICATION

When God gives you creative gifts, He expects you use them. In order to use your gifts, you must first understand what they are and how they operate. In other words, you must spend time nurturing them. Depending on your gifts, nurturing may involve going to school, taking lessons, practicing your craft, identifying a mentor, etc. When you engage in such activities, you are further developing what God has given you in an effort to make sure that you are well equipped to use it. The more you develop and nurture your gifts, the more powerful they become, and the greater impact they will have in the Kingdom.

When you recognize the creative gifts that God has given you, it is important not to become proud and boastful. The gifts are for the Kingdom, not for your personal gratification. Yes, you will often be recognized for your gifts, but it is important in those moments to remind people that you are a servant of God, utilizing the gifts that He has bestowed upon you for His glory, not your own.

Those who never devote time to nurturing their creative gifts and, ultimately, do not use their gifts send two messages to God. The first is that they are not thankful for that which He has given. The second message is that they do not desire to have their gifts used by and for God. When God distributes gifts, each gift and each person who possesses it is a part of a greater plan. Those who choose not to use the gifts, by default, choose to not participate in the plan and to not complete the assignments that are a part of fulfilling God's purpose for their lives. There is no greater joy than living your life on purpose and according to His plan. I encourage you to nurture and use your God-given gifts!

PRAYER

Father, I thank You for the creative gifts that You have placed within me. I commit to nurturing and using these gifts to the best of my ability and for the purposes You have set forth. I will increase my knowledge about my gifts and all things related so that Your power is manifested through them. I vow not to allow my gifts to lie dormant. I will use them actively for Your glory. I ask for a spirit of humbleness so that I direct the praises that I receive for the use of my gifts to You. It is not my desire to consider myself greater than others because You have chosen to bless me with these gifts. I thank You for choosing me, recognizing that we are all Your children and equal in Your eyes. Amen.

DAY 3

UNDERSTANDING YOUR CREATIVE WORTH

Are you comparing yourself and your gifts to others?

"Having then gifts differing according to the grace that is given to us, whether prophecy, let us prophesy according to the proportion of faith."
(ROMANS 12:6)

STORY

As time went on, Charles gave Carol additional responsibilities, but a portion of her responsibilities always remained assisting him in some way. One day, Charles walked into Carol's office and

told her that he had a proposition for her. Carol was immediately excited because this usually meant that the organization had received a grant for a new program. She never expected what Charles said next.

"I'd like for you to serve as Director of Operations," he said with excitement.

"Of what operations?" she asked.

"Of all operations within the organization. You will be the second in charge and my right hand. I think you're ready."

"I don't know if I am," Carol responded. "I haven't been here as long as others. What will they think if you promote me and not them?"

"They will think that I made a good choice. I need you to KNOW that I have made a good choice. From your first day until now, you have shown your commitment to the organization and your belief in its mission. You have contributed greatly with your creative ideas and administrative skills. I have been grooming you for this position for a while. Don't worry about others; believe in yourself and take every opportunity to utilize your gifts!"

Carol accepted the position. She asked God to increase her confidence so that she would recognize the worth of the creative gifts she possessed. She wanted to believe in herself!

APPLICATION

Your gift is your voice for God. Though several people may have been blessed with the same type of gift, in each individual's hands, the gift is unique and has its own purpose. Think of the many singers and musicians in the world. They all have been gifted with a voice and/or the ability to play instruments, but the sounds that they produce are their own. We easily recognize their unique voices and styles of music without ever seeing their faces. Each has been gifted to reach a specific audience. God has already identified those who will be blessed by your gifts.

Be careful not to fall into the trap of comparing yourself and your creative gifts to others. When God gave you gifts, He knew that they would be uniquely yours. The uniqueness of your gift is the creativity that you apply to it. Everything that makes you who you are is manifested in the delivery of your gifts to the world. These are YOUR creative gifts; they are not supposed look, sound, feel, or manifest themselves in the same manner as someone else's gifts. Therefore, stop comparing yourself and your gifts to others! Your gifts are intended to touch the lives of designated people at the designated time for a designated purpose. Instead of focusing on others, focus on what is unique about your creative gifts from God and use that uniqueness to glorify Him!

PRAYER

Lord, thank You for all of the things that make me who I am. I appreciate the gifts that You have blessed me with, and I realize that You chose me for a reason. Therefore, I will use these gifts to the best of my ability to touch the lives of others. Please forgive me if I have compared myself and my gifts to others. What You blessed others with is for them and what You blessed me with is for me. I will celebrate the gifts of others and never covet them. Open my eyes to the creativity within me that makes my gifts unique and all my own. Give me the confidence to believe in myself. I am forever grateful to You for all that You have done for me. Amen.

DAY 4
KNOWING GOD'S MIGHTY PLANS

Have you determined your Kingdom assignments?

"For it is God which worketh in you both to will and to do of his good pleasure."
(PHILIPPIANS 2:13)

STORY

Carol excelled in her new role. She was an outstanding leader and manager. Eventually, her confidence increased and she became comfortable being in charge. Her passion never diminished; it increased. She created new programs that gained local, regional, and national attention. When she initially began working for the nonprofit, she never envisioned her work reaching beyond the geographical boundaries of her hometown. She never imagined that her work would draw the interest of many and that her expertise would be sought after to help others do similar work. Because of her creative gifts, Carol testified before Congress and traveled the world sharing with others positive ways to affect the lives of economically disadvantaged people by providing them educational and job opportunities.

The smiles on the faces of those who benefited from her work meant the world to Carol. She truly believed that God had given her the gift of administration, and she envisioned herself in this role forever. In her mind, she had discovered and mastered her God-given assignments. Then, life happened.

APPLICATION

There is much work to be done in the Kingdom of God, work that requires creativity in thought and deed. In order to ensure that His work on earth is accomplished, God uses His people. The Kingdom assignments that God has determined for your life are directly related to the creative gifts that He has placed within you. In His infinite wisdom, God has a set purpose for all of His believers. He has developed assignments for them to complete and equipped them to accomplish that which He desires. However, many of us have not determined or do not know how to determine our Kingdom assignments.

In school, the teacher gives an assignment after teaching the information, knowledge, and skills necessary to complete it. The teacher is there to provide direction, answer questions, and further assist students in their efforts. The students each bring their own creative approach and their personal experiences to the assignments. As students progress, their assignments become more difficult and expanded knowledge is required to complete them. This same concept applies to our Kingdom assignments. In order to determine and complete our Kingdom assignments, we must go to the Master Teacher.

From the time we accept Jesus Christ as our Savior, God begins to nurture, develop, and teach us. He teaches us about Him, and He teaches us about ourselves. He reveals to us our positive traits as well as our negative traits. He reveals to us what is special about us, our creative gifts, and His purpose for our lives. He forgives us for our actions that do not align with His word and His expectations of us as Christians. He shows us how to become more like Him. As God nurtures, develops, and teaches us, He is preparing us for our Kingdom assignments, those designed by Him, specifically for us.

We will have many assignments throughout our lives. Each of us can determine our Kingdom assignments through our communication with God. He knows exactly what He needs us to do for His good pleasure. God will give us the creative ideas and concepts to complete the assignments. Seek God, the Master Teacher!

PRAYER

Lord, thank You for choosing me to serve You. It is my desire to know the plans that You have for my life. I want to complete the Kingdom assignments that You designed specifically for me. Recognizing that the Kingdom is waiting for me to do my part, I surrender myself to You so that You may direct my path. Teach me, oh Lord, how to tap into the creative gifts that You have placed within me. Show me how to incorporate these gifts into my Kingdom assignments. Continue to show me how I can become more like You as I prepare to do Your will. From this day forward, I will open my mind and heart to recognizing opportunities for me to complete my Kingdom assignments. Amen.

RECOGNIZING A GIFT'S MAGNITUDE

Have you prepared yourself for greatness?

"A man's gift maketh room for him, and bringeth him before great men."
(PROVERBS 18:16)

STORY

Carol battled addiction. She overcame her struggles through her faith in God. She stood on His promises and He delivered her. After this experience, God instructed Carol to use her gifts for a new assignment, helping others overcome addiction. She was grateful for the new assignment and it became her passion. She combined all that she had learned as an administrator with what she had experienced as an addict and established Hope House, a nonprofit organization that offered services to recovering addicts. The Hope House recovery program was built on the foundation of God's promises.

Carol's work with Hope House made a difference in her community. Her programs and commitment were once again recognized locally, regionally, and nationally. She received service awards for her commitment. Participants sang her praises. The program was so successful that it was replicated nationwide. Hope House became synonymous with addiction recovery, and it established an army of recovering addicts on a mission to help others.

When she took her first job as an administrative assistant, Carol had no knowledge of the creative gifts within her nor the assignments that God had pre-ordained for her to complete. By seeking Him, she discovered her gifts, nurtured them, and tackled her assignments one by one. As she experienced life's ups and downs, she continued to communicate with God and never stopped using her gifts to glorify Him.

While preparing her remarks to accept the Making a Difference Outstanding Award for Service from the Congressional Black Caucus, Carol was overwhelmed by the realization that her gifts had made room for her and bestowed upon her recognition by great men and women. She thanked God for her journey from discovering her creative gifts to using them to make a difference!

APPLICATION

Often times, when we discover our creative gifts and the purposes for which God has given them, we are excited and eager to use them. Many times, we use them as often as we can, without much notice from others. Because of our love for God, we constantly desire our gifts to have a greater impact on the Kingdom and to touch larger numbers of people. There are times we begin to question if we are using our gifts properly and according to God's plan. Know that God's plan and promises to you will be fulfilled at the appropriate time.

How many times have you watched an old movie and recognized a now famous actor? More than likely, you thought to yourself, "I didn't realize he had been an actor for so long." You did not realize it because most actors must work their way to notoriety by large audiences. Just because only a few people know of your creative gifts now does not mean that your gift will not make room for you and garner the attention of many.

You can rest assured that God's plan for you and your creative gifts is much greater than what you could ask or think. When it is time for your gifts to receive recognition and have a major impact on the Kingdom, God will connect you with the right people. Wait on the Lord. They that wait on the Lord shall renew their strength if they faint not. God gave you the gift, and it will make room for you!

PRAYER

Lord, thank You for my journey. I am grateful for the ups and the downs as well as the joys and disappointments because all of these experiences have brought me to this place. This is the place where I am fully aware of the creative gifts that You have placed within me. In this place, I am clear about the assignments that You would have me to complete. Here, I am aware of the importance of staying in constant communication with You. Today, Lord, I can say with confidence that my gifts have made room for me. I know that I would not have had the opportunities to stand before great men and women had it not been for You. I bless You with my whole heart and recommit my gifts to You. As long as You have an assignment for me, I stand ready to complete it. Amen.

JUNE
WEEK 3

DAY 1
A LOVING FATHER

Do you show love to others?

"For all the law is fulfilled in one word, even in this; Thou shalt love thy neighbour as thyself."
(GALATIANS 5:14)

STORY

Our neighborhood was like a village where everyone knew each other. Every adult had the approval to discipline a child found doing wrong, and the child knew to expect another whipping from their parents when they got home. One home was the exception because my friend Judy's parents treated us as if no child could do wrong. Her father, Hank, spent time not only talking and teaching us about life but also playing with us. When we needed a toy worked on or fixed, all of the children of the village knew that Hank would take care of it.

It was amazing to see how loving this man was with his wife and children. Just as soon as he got home each evening from work, his children would all but tackle him to the ground, jumping and hugging on him. Judy would giggle and scream as her loving father would pick her up, throw her up in the air, catch her in his big arms, and then land a smacking kiss on her face. That really showed love to all of us; in fact, sometimes Hank would hug all of us to make sure we felt his love.

APPLICATION

The world is comprised of many families, races, cultures, and communities. The one thing common among us all is showing affection. A hug and kiss always means the same everywhere and to all humankind. God shows His love to humankind every day. He blesses us beyond the daily mercy and grace that He bestows on us each new day. The least we can do in return is to share love with others, including those in our homes and those we encounter as we go about our daily lives. We especially should share love with those who choose to mistreat us.

Jesus was given to the world through love from the Father to show us real love. He gave us the commandment to love each other and then to love our neighbors as ourselves. That scripture requires that first we love ourselves. Then, we show our appreciation for His love by sharing our love with others each day.

PRAYER

Dear Lord, I thank You for the greatest love that was demonstrated when You gave Your son to this world. Jesus, I thank You for Your love shown as You left heaven to live on earth as a man and die as a sinner on a cross. Yet, You won victory over death and power through Your resurrection to give us eternal life with the Father. You did not have to do it, but You did! Teach me to give sacrificial and unconditional love with all that I encounter on a daily basis. I desire to give absolute love that demonstrates the love of God in my everyday walk and talk. Let others see You through my daily life and exemplary love. This, I pray, in the name of Jesus, Amen.

DAY 2

A FEARFUL FATHER

Do you fear your father and God?

"The Lord is my light and my salvation;
whom shall I fear? the LORD is the strength of my life;
of whom shall I be afraid?"
(PSALM 27:1)

STORY

As we grew into our teenager years, the gossip of the neighborhood led us to believe that Judy's father had been caught sleeping around. Her parents' relationship suffered, and soon she found herself being raised by a single mom. The children of the neighborhood lost their friend Hank because he moved out of town. We could always tell when Hank was expected to come for

a visit because Judy's face would just gleam with smiles when she shared with us her plans for Hank's visit.

There was an unexpected visit one weekend when we were at Judy's house for a slumber party. Hank came in upset about something. At first, we just heard arguing, but then it turned into more, and we heard furniture being knocked over and thrown. We were all afraid to leave Judy's bedroom. None of us had ever experienced such fear in our lives. As we hugged and trembled, tears just streamed down Judy's face. Not only was she embarrassed for us to witness this behavior, but she kept praying that he would not come into the bedroom where we had actually hidden together in the closet.

APPLICATION

God does not want us to be afraid of Him or even man. I was not afraid of my father because I knew he was always there to take care of me. Yet, I did live with the fear of what he might say or do if I chose to be disrespectful or dishonest in a situation. Since I did not want to suffer the punishment he might give, I was usually not found doing stuff that would get me in trouble, such as not getting home after school at the expected time or, heaven forbid, doing something wrong in school that caused the teacher to call home to report me.

It is the same with our lives and our relationship with God. I challenge you not to be afraid of God. Sometimes we do not make wise choices, especially when we live in fear that we are all alone. We should live each day with an assurance that God is always present to take care of us. Yes, you can lean and depend on Him for your every need and the desires of your heart, like the new car you want. I am fearful to think just what I would be or do without God. Will I be ready when He calls for me on the day of judgement or the day He returns for His own?

PRAYER

Our Father, which art in heaven, thank You for just being my father. You are the one who knows me just as my earthly fathers know me. Thank You for the good father You provided to raise me to be a good daughter to him and to You. Bless my mind and deeds so that they are pure and holy, not of evil or forsaking others. Deliver me from any moments of fear that make me think that You are not present. In these days of wars and rumors of wars, let me not be afraid of man nor his weapons but assured that You will protect me and keep me, as any good father would do for his children and family. In the name of Jesus, Amen.

DAY 3
A LISTENING FATHER

Do people listen to you?

"Seek good, and not evil, that ye may live: and so the LORD, the God of hosts, shall be with you, as ye have spoken."
(AMOS 5:14)

STORY

After the program with music, scripture, and prayer was presented for our Family and Friends Day at church, it was time for the real deal, which was eating. Many people brought food, but there were some mothers whose food everyone wanted to sample. Judy's mother and grandmother had the best chicken and dumplings, greens, potato pies, and coconut cake. There was growing commotion as many tried to get to their table. The noise level was rising as people began to shove and push trying to get a good spot at the table. Judy even felt the table rocking as a couple of people tussled for their position in the line. It finally took her father, Hank, to get the crowd's attention; you see when that man spoke everyone listened. He had a deep voice that just demanded attention even with the kindest comment being given. Growing up, if there seemed to be a fight among the children playing Hank could just raise his voice and all would listen. Who would have even thought that Christians would all but be fighting over a piece of pie? Judy and Hank moved from behind the table to the front to greet people individually and assure them that they would be served.

APPLICATION

The old proverb, "Sticks and stones will break my bones, but words will never hurt me." is so untrue. Words not only hurt but also destroy feelings, friendships, relationships, and even situations. What we say is always important because you never know just who might be listening. Many times things are said and others listening do not know the whole story and will then form wrong opinions because things may have been taken out of context or meaning. That is even more of a reason to seek good and not evil because good words will never hurt someone.

In the story of Job, his wife told him to curse God and die. Job knew that there were others watching, waiting, and listening to hear him complain of what God had allowed to be done to him. Job was determined not to have others believe that he had lost his faith. He responded to his wife by questioning her faith.

Jesus commanded us to love our neighbors as ourselves. This, we must do even when we may want to speak evil of someone. Remember that God is listening. He is omniscient for He knows all even before anything is said. We can communicate with Him in prayer for He listens to our every thought, action, and deed. He is present. Call on Him. Indeed, He will answer for He listens.

PRAYER

Oh Lord, my creator, I thank You for always being present and listening. You listen to my thoughts even before they are spoken, and You hear my voice as speech goes forth. Clean my heart and mind so Your Holy Spirit may abide in me to purify my thoughts and speech. Lord, use me and speak through me so others will hear of Your goodness and understand that You are forever present in our daily lives. Thank You for the armor of God that daily shields me from the evilness of this world. Keep my ears and eyes open to see and hear as You speak to me and through me. Let me be an instrument of peace to help those who may be listening to my voice and need a reminder that You are omniscient and forever present to lead, guide, and protect me. Let the words of my mouth and the meditation of my heart be acceptable unto You so that only goodness comes from my words to those who may be listening. In the name of Jesus, I pray, Amen.

DAY 4
A DEPENDABLE FATHER

Who do you depend on?

"Trust in the Lord with all thine heart;
and lean not unto thine own understanding."
(PROVERBS 3:5)

STORY

Frustration was all in the air as the family gathered waiting on a call. Judy had received a text message from her brother's friend that he had been arrested. It did not say what the circumstances were or what was necessary to get him out of jail. There had been much unrest in the city since the recent killing of a young black male who was accused of running from a store

where the storeowner said there had been a robbery. If that were not enough, Judy was having issues at work and pondering whether she should file sexual harassment charges against her boss or just quit her job.

Many times in the past, Judy had gone to her father, Hank, for help. She depended on her father but really did not want to bother him with everything going on with her brother. However, just as she had leaned and depended on Hank in the past, she was confident that he would help her think through things. The experience and wisdom of Hank always seemed to be just what she needed. He would give her options that would lead to sound resolutions.

APPLICATION

We do not always understand just why things happen the way they do. In fact, an old hymn tells us "we will understand it better by and by." We go to work every day thinking we are doing just fine, only later to find out that someone may be plotting against us. Do you not know that Satan is at work doing his job daily to distract and destroy our relationship with God? When we lose our faith and trust in God, even for just a minute, we think we can do everything for ourselves, and all will be just fine.

That might be true if there were no Satan hard at work against us. That is why we must daily pray to God for His direction and guidance. Sometimes, we may even need another soldier on the battlefield of life with us. Thank God for loving and dependable parents and family members who will pray with us. In our relationship with God, we must be confident that regardless of the storms in life, God is omnipotent and all powerful. He is omnipresent, and He is always with us. Know that He will forever be with us. It is up to you to trust Him and lean not unto your own understanding, but lean and depend on God.

PRAYER

Father, I praise Your name for You are my rock of salvation. Thank You for sending Your son Jesus to die for my sins and giving me what I need to prepare for everlasting life with You. Thank You for the Holy Spirit that has been sent to be my comforter when needed. Yes, Lord, there are times that I do not understand why things are happening all around me. I don't understand war, people killing each other or people engaging in human trafficking, racism, discrimination, and harassment for no apparent reason. Beyond the lack of my understanding, I plead forgiveness of my sins. Thank You for being there for me daily to lean and depend on during my time of slumber and my time awake. I believe in Your word when You said that You would never leave nor forsake me. I thank You now for being a fence of protection around me, shielding me from evil and protecting me when I might do something that would bring harm to myself. Keep me in Your care forever. This, I pray in the name of Jesus, Amen.

DAY 5

A STANDING FATHER

Will you take a stand?

*"Only let your conversation be as it becometh
the gospel of Christ: that whether I come and see you,
or else be absent, I may hear of your affairs,
that ye stand fast in one spirit, with one mind striving
together for the faith of the gospel."*
(PHILIPPIANS 1:27)

STORY

Some decisions in our life come with pain and suffering. We all want the best that life has to offer but sometimes that means dealing with people and even circumstances that look like situations will not be in our favor.

There was a job opening that Judy knew she had more than the credentials required for the position. She already had job experiences that prepared her to walk into the job ready. She understood that to apply for the position might raise questions of her wanting to leave her current job area. There were oppositions in her path such as her race and even her gender; no African American woman had ever served as the County Administrator.

Judy wanted the job for not only the promising pay increase but also to have the opportunity to provide needed assistance to many African American families in her community. Her family, especially her father and friends, encouraged her to apply, trust that she would get the job, and just wait to see the outcome. What happened? Judy is now the County Administrator.

APPLICATION

God does not always give us gifts because we deserve them. Sometimes, we have to withstand the added pressures of life and stand steadfast in our belief that what God has for us it is for us. Many people go through life waiting on a better tomorrow and thinking that because they are a good person, God will just drop them the blessing of a new job or position. However, we must do our part and prepare ourselves to meet the challenge. Yes, God opens windows of opportunities and doors to success every day, but often this requires action on our parts to be in the right position to receive the blessing. Sitting a plate of food in front of a starving man does nothing until the man takes action and eats the food.

We must be willing to stand on the word of God. Standing on His word means believing in His promises. God will do exactly what He said He would do if you simply stand.

PRAYER

Oh God, my heavenly Father, thank You for being omnipotent and using Your power for my good. Lord, You have watched over me since conception, and I thank You. I may not have done all things just right as You commanded, but I pray that You will continue to bless me each day with new mercies and grace. For I know with Your mercy and grace that I can stand in victory as I face the evilness of this world. I know You have all power over any weapon that may be formed to bring harm to me, be it missiles, guns, or even arrows of hatred shot my way in someone's deeds or actions. Lord, let Your love so abide in me that others may see You through me. As I go from day to day, use me to do Your will and show others the way to salvation and Your prepared eternal home for believers. Thank You for Your son who said that He was going to prepare a place for my eternal resting. Stand by me and guide me. I pray in the name of Jesus, Amen.

JUNE
WEEK 4

DAY 1
WITH OUR LORD

How can you increase your time with the Lord?

"God is faithful, who has called you into fellowship with his Son, Jesus Christ our Lord."
(I CORINTHIANS 1:9, NIV)

STORY

The first official day on the campus of Spelman College, Kali looked around in amazement that she was a college freshman. She and her parents, exhausted from the long trip and setting up her dorm room, heard loud noises. Click, bang, boom! Her roommate stumbled through the door and tripped into the lap of Kali's mom as she stored sweaters

underneath Kali's bed. Emoni apologized profusely, and Kali introduces herself and her parents, the Norwoods.

Kali's dad shared that it is very late, and they must get on the road. Emoni watched as they immediately drew near to one another and embraced each other's hands. Kali looked over at Emoni and asked if she would like to join them in prayer.

Not knowing how she should respond, Emoni stated, "Sure, why not?"

Emoni noticed something about Kali. Before she went to sleep, she kneeled at her bed and prayed. Before she consumed food, she prayed. Before she rose from a night's sleep, she prayed. Before she took a test, she prayed. Emoni could tell that even while sitting quietly in their room sometimes, Kali was praying.

"What's up with this girl?" Emoni thought.

APPLICATION

In 1988, Tina Turner's "Break Every Rule World Tour" achieved one of the highest attendee levels ever at 180,000 for single artist ticketed concerts. That same year Michael Jackson's "Bad World Tour" pulled in over 125,000 attendees. People could not wait to get in the presence of Tina and Michael, to hear their voices, marvel at their talent and be in awe of the energy they brought to those arenas.

While extremely impressive, those numbers pale in comparison to the greatest of all time. There will never be any greater than the great "I am." The most precious gift that goes beyond all that we could possibly imagine receiving is to commune with God. You do not have to wait in long lines, pull out your credit card, or yell across thousands of people hoping He hears your voice. He hears the soft whispers from your lips, the shout-outs because of joy and pain, the silent pleas for help, the praises for answered prayers, and the why questions for perceived injustices.

God hears you loud and clear. His desire is to spend time with you, and He rejoices when you come to Him. Fellowship with God is having an intimate relationship with Him. When you commune constantly, His ways become your ways. His purpose and desires become your purpose and desires. Whenever you have questions, you can ask the Lord and He answers. His answers give us peace concerning all of the details of our daily lives.

PRAYER

Heavenly Father, I am grateful that I can come to You in all things. You are my sovereign Father, He who knew me before the foundation of the world. There is nothing too small or big for You to handle. Your ever-present help is with me always. I ask that You lead, guide, and direct my path through everything that life brings my way. In Jesus' name, Amen.

DAY 2
WITH OUR ACTIONS

How are your actions aligned with His word?

"If we claim to have fellowship with him and yet walk in the darkness, we lie and do not live out the truth. But if we walk in the light, as he is in the light, we have fellowship with one another, and the blood of Jesus, his Son, purifies us from all sin."

(I JOHN 1:6-7, NIV)

STORY

After the first day of class, both Kali and Emoni obtained their class syllabi and raced to the bookstore to get the best deals on used books. They were told by the upperclassmen that they would pay too much if they waited too long. Neither young woman could understand why the

69

professors did not simply assign books that were digital anyway, but go figure!

As they walked up to the store, Kali noticed a very frail young woman hovered toward the corner of the building. They both went in and began to gather their respective books. Emoni was taken aback totally by the amount of money her books cost, and this was much more than Kali expected as well.

While checking out, Kali noticed the young woman they saw outside the store was now in the store crying in the corner. She went over to see what was wrong, and the young woman explained she did not have enough money to get the last book she needed for class and have money to eat for the week. Kali had her come to check out with her, and she purchased the young woman's book.

Emoni looked at Kali in amazement and thought, "Who is this girl?"

APPLICATION

Jesus' mother gave explicit instructions to the wedding attendant to do whatever Jesus instructed. As a result, the bridegroom and bride, along with their guests, experienced the first recorded miracle of Jesus when He turned water into wine. Mary trusted Jesus; it was evident by her actions. As she fellowshipped with others, she encouraged them to trust Him as well.

I have heard many say, "I'd rather see a sermon than hear a sermon." In other words, let your actions demonstrate the word of God that is in your heart. Your actions should align with the commandments of God. You are the light of the world. A city set on a hill cannot be hidden. People should see your actions and give glory to the Father in Heaven.

Is that happening in your life? Are you living life in such a way that it gives glory to the Father? If not, you need to work on it. Mary is telling us to do whatever Jesus tells us to do. It is imperative that we hear His word, then go, and do as He has instructed us to do. Let your light shine before men that they may see your good works and give glory to God.

P R A Y E R

Father God, forgive me of any wrong I may have done. Cleanse my heart so that I may go and do the work You have called me to do. Lord, You knew me before I was formed in my mother's womb. I pray that the sharing of my faith may become effective for the full knowledge of every good thing that is in me for the sake of You. Thank You for never leaving me nor abandoning me. Your presence brings my heart joy. Cast out anything from me, Father, that is not like You. In Jesus' name, Amen.

DAY 3

WITH ONE ANOTHER

How can God use you to love your brothers and sisters?

"We proclaim to you what we have seen and heard, so that you also may have fellowship with us. And our fellowship is with the Father and with his Son, Jesus Christ. We write this to make our joy complete."

(I JOHN 1:3-4, NIV)

STORY

Midterms were a beast. Both Kali and Emoni were feeling the heat. They both were strong academically; however, Emoni wondered if she had taken on more than she could handle. Kali did not allow her roommate to get discouraged.

She shared study techniques with her, drilled her on her course materials, created notecards, and even taped them to her roommate's mirror for visual reinforcement.

Kali invited Emoni out to her study group session to break the monotony of their dorm room. As they were walking to the library, Emoni asked if this session was with her chemistry, Spanish, or calculus peers. Kali smiled and there was a level of peace that resided in her.

"No, I've built an alliance of high performing students of various majors, and we meet to make each other better," Kali shared.

As they enter the conference room, Emoni choose to take a seat in the corner. She began to notice that even extremely brilliant students still have areas of study that they need help with studying. She could not believe Kali needed help in solving a calculus problem, but she did!

APPLICATION

All of us are objects of God's love. He has placed us here for fellowship with one another. As our spirits connect, we, as a collective, become better. Fellowship with one another is iron sharpening iron, as one man sharpens another. Each of us has been given specific spiritual gifts. When we come together in fellowship, we are demonstrating God's power together.

Can you imagine a cake without flour, sugar, eggs, or oil? The eggs will never be the flour; they have their own distinct role to play in the creation of the cake. As God's children, so do we.

It takes the sum of the parts to make the whole! The body of Christ is one and has many members. All of the members of the body, though many, are one body. We must be committed to spending time together, urging, inspiring, praying, rebuking, partaking in God's word, as well as praying over God's word and the necessities of our church, so that we become sharper and more cutting in the ministry that the Lord has assigned to each of us.

Washing that spot at the center of your back is too great to bear alone. It is much better to have fellowship with another to help cleanse those dirty areas. Simply put, connect with fellow believers to help each other to become better. We must lift up others before the crisis comes, so they are well prepared to weather any storm.

PRAYER

Almighty Father, give me the heart and strength to bear another's burden. You took the weight of this world so I might have eternal life with You. You first loved me, and for that, I am ever grateful. I thank You for the fellowship with others, with the You and Your son, Jesus Christ. I am delighted and overjoyed by the touching of my spirit with fellow believers. I ask that You reveal my spiritual talents so that I may use them to uplift Your Kingdom. In Jesus' name, Amen.

DAY 4
WITH OUR SELF

*How has God gotten you through
some tough times?*

*"Therefore, I urge you, brothers and sisters, in view
of God's mercy, to offer your bodies as a living
sacrifice, holy and pleasing to God—this is your
true and proper worship."*
(ROMANS 12:1, NIV)

STORY

As the alarm sounded at 7 a.m., Emoni
rolled over and realized Kali was not
there.

"Uhm, gone again," Emoni said to herself.
"I don't know how she does it all. She was

up until 3 a.m. studying for her chemistry exam, and she's gone already."

Emoni jumped up, ran to the shower. When she returned, Kali was back.

Emoni asked, "Where do you go multiple times a week before dawn?"

Kali explained that there is a food pantry on campus where shipments come in on Monday, Wednesday, and Friday's, and she receives the food and stocks the shelves for the homeless and hungry.

"That explains it! You are sacrificing a lot of sleep to do that, and speaking of food, I've been told that typically freshmen put on fifteen pounds. You seem to be disappearing."

Emoni told Kali that she had not seen her eat anything in two weeks. All of sudden there was a knock at the door. A young woman stood there, sharing that she was collecting shoes for a local children's homeless shelter. Kali immediately ran to her closet, grabbed five pairs of her shoes, and thrust them in the box.

Emoni yelled, "Hold it! You just bought some of those shoes."

Kali smiled and said, "I can get more. The children at the shelter need them more than I do."

APPLICATION

Taking a good hard look at ourselves and facing our flaws can be a struggle. Our relationship with God requires us to fellowship with Him on a spiritual level that causes us to make significant sacrifices. By reading the Bible and worshipping God, we are penetrating the soil of our hearts and minds to receive the seed of eternal life with God. As the gardener toils his land to develop the perfect green grass, so must we continue to minister to ourselves in the development of a strong relationship with God.

When a gardener fertilizes the ground, he prepares it to receive the seed. In many cases, weeds may rear their ugly heads, and the gardener has to extinguish them. We must do the same. When the body begins to desire things that are of the world, we must institute our weeding process called fasting and confession of scripture. When the sacrifice of ourselves to God is holy, it is acceptable and pleasing to God. The sacrifice of ourselves to God is our reasonable service.

PRAYER

Lord God, give me the strength to do nothing from rivalry or conceit, but in humility, count others more significant than myself. I shall pay careful attention to myself and to all whom the Holy Spirit has placed in my life to care for in the church of God, which He obtained with His own blood. I ask that You continually watch over me and think through my mind. Make my actions be aligned with Your will and Your ways. Let my heart sing praises of You at all times. In Jesus' name, Amen.

DAY 5

WITH OUR TONGUE

How have you used words to uplift someone lately?

"Do not let any unwholesome talk come out of your mouths, but only what is helpful for building others up according to their needs, that it may benefit those who listen."
(EPHESIANS 4:29, NIV)

STORY

Standing in front of the student center, hanging out with some of their friends, Kali and Emoni overheard their friends calling one young woman outlandish and harsh names. The condemned friend dropped her head and began to cry.

Kali leaned over to her, brushed her hair back and said, "You and I both know none of those names fit you, and none of those lies are true."

Kali then began to share with the other young women all of the times the condemned friend was at each of their sides when they needed a friend.

"Sonya, when your mom got sick, and you needed to get home that evening, who took you? Melissa, when you were sick with the flu, who made your meals and got your medicine? Allison, who tutored you in math all semester to ensure that you passed the class? Summer, who threw you an 18th birthday party because she wanted you happy since it was the first time you were away from your twin on your birthday? Felicia, who served as your campaign manager and led your victorious quest as Miss Freshman? If given a chance, she could be a great friend to the rest of you too."

Emoni took a deep breath and exclaimed, "Now, I get it. She is a child of the Most High God!"

APPLICATION

Oh, how sweet it is! There is a tropical West African plant called "miracle fruit," which contains a chemical that affects taste receptors in the tongue. This chemical makes the tongue register sour tastes as sweet tastes. It binds itself strongly with the sweet taste buds on your tongue and is activated when there is a change in the pH level of your mouth, which is when you taste something sour or bitter. Your brain temporarily identifies sour and bitter flavors as sweet due to this.

The Bible tells us that pleasant words are as a honeycomb, sweet to the soul and health to the bones. Just imagine if you were able to taste this fruit before every encounter with a hostile customer, a bad driver who cuts you off, the uptight boss who refuses to give you a break, or that neighbor who refuses to stop playing loud music at 3 a.m. every morning. As God's children, we are to let no corrupt talk come out of our mouths but only such as is good for building up that it may give grace to those who hear.

As we fellowship with our Father through prayer, fasting, studying His word, and obeying His commandments, we begin to see Him becoming the sweet foundation of our tongues. The presence of rude, hostile, disrespectable, arrogant, and sour people who have had trouble in their lives does not cause us to reject them in bitter disgust but shower them with kindness, gentleness, thoughtfulness, and uplifting words to soothe their souls.

PRAYER

Heavenly Father, You spoke this world into existence, everything that You said was done. Set a guard, O Lord, over my mouth; keep watch over the door of my lips! Keep my tongue from evil and my lips from speaking deceit. Let my speech always be gracious, seasoned with salt, so that I may know how I ought to answer each person. As I open my mouth, let it be with wisdom, and let the teaching of kindness be on my tongue. Let me pursue what makes for peace and mutual uplifting. In Jesus' name, Amen.

JULY
WEEK 5

DAY 1
WISDOM IS STRENGTH

Is wisdom your guide?

"The fear of the LORD is the beginning of knowledge: but fools despise wisdom and instruction."
(PROVERBS 1:7)

STORY

Wisdom is defined as knowledge and ability. Wisdom is knowing what is right and doing it. It has the power to change things through thinking. It will ease stress and cause less worry. It will give a peace like no other. It will allow one to see the beauty of God's love. Wisdom is swallowing pride as well as knowing when to walk away and simply be still. Wisdom is a state of mind. Wisdom is knowledge rightfully applied.

There was a little girl named Keisa who lived by a small white church with a cross on the top. She began to play, and the more she played the further she drifted away from home. All of a sudden, Keisa realized she was lost and began to wander. Fear began to set in, and she said quietly to herself, "If I can find my way back to the cross, then I can find my way back home."

APPLICATION

God freely gives wisdom to all who ask. In the Bible, the Lord appeared to Solomon in a dream and asked him what he desired. Solomon asked for an understanding heart to judge the people so he could discern between good and bad. Because Solomon did not ask for long life, riches for himself, or harm for his enemies, God was pleased and gave him the desires of his heart.

Just like Solomon, each day we should ask God in a daily prayer to provide us with an understanding heart and discernment. Wisdom and discernment are the willingness to experience the world through His eyes so that knowledge can be acquired and rightfully applied.

PRAYER

Awesome God, continue to pour out Your wisdom on all humankind. Father, continue to allow Your word to convict, strengthen, teach, and heal. Help me to come boldly to You for wisdom and knowledge in all that I say and do. Let it become as normal to me as the air I breathe. It is with wisdom that the world can become a better place. Let Your wisdom have its way. Let it lead, carry, and guide me always. In Jesus name, Amen.

DAY 2

WISDOM IS INSIGHT

What do you do when you do not have the answer?

"The way of a fool is right in his own eyes: but he that hearkeneth unto counsel is wise."
(PROVERBS 12:15)

STORY

Has there ever been a situation in life that did not make sense. Did it raise many questions of how and why? Did it began to consume every thought?

Kesia met the man of her dreams. He promised her the world, and everything she asked for she was given. She thought her life was well put together. She was in love and living what

she thought was her best life until her boyfriend began using verbal put-downs, criticizing her, and making negative comments. One day, during a general conversation, he became agitated and pushed her. She brushed it off as him being temporarily disgruntled. She did not realize this was the beginning of stages of physical abuse, which she had never experienced in her life. Kesia ignored it, and it got progressively worse. The decisions she made were based on her feelings and her being in what she thought was love.

The abuse escalated to a level of fear. She knew she had to leave, but she could not begin to fathom how. While journaling to God one day, He began to speak the answer to her. He told her that the situation was not her fault or her choice. The relationship was a deception of what love really is. Sometimes, we have to experience what love is not in order to actually feel what it is. God told her to trust His will for her life and to stand on His word. He reassured her that all things will work together for her good and His glory. The weapons may form, but they will not prosper. He has the final say. She got herself together and found the courage and strength to leave the relationship. She forgave her ex-boyfriend and never looked back.

APPLICATION

God gives us wisdom to get through our toughest situations in life. In the Bible, Abigail showed wisdom when she had to deal with a surly and mean husband along with a very angry and revengeful David. Abigail used what she learned in her relationship with God and applied that wisdom in dealing with her husband Nabal and David. Because of her wisdom and obedience to God, David listened to her and did not retaliate.

In life, at times we value human wisdom instead of God's wisdom. The minute a problem arises or we need a quick answer, we tend to call a friend. This may work sometimes, but God is the source of true wisdom. He wants us to bring our problems to the altar and surrender them to Him. God wants to be the one to hear our problems and solve them. He wants His will to be done. His answer and solution will flow in love, peace, and harmony. He knows what is best above what we think we know and feel. God recognizes every outcome to every situation before it even begins. It is God's all-knowing power and His will for our lives that make all things work together for the good of those called according to His purpose. God's word will always provide guidance and peace when we are facing the most difficult challenges. Be wise and seek His guidance in all you do.

PRAYER

Father, in You there is wisdom, knowledge, understanding, and discernment. Let me not make any decisions moving forward without first seeking Your wisdom. If I seek You first, my life would be a lot more peaceful and stress free. You are the answer to all questions. I ask You to speak to my heart and give me wisdom. Have Your way! Amen.

DAY 3

WISDOM IS POWER

God, where are You?

"If any of you lack wisdom, let him ask of God, that giveth to all men liberally, and upbraideth not; and it shall be given him."

(JAMES 1:5)

STORY

There are times when the questions "God, where are You?" and "Can You hear me?" are asked. In those times, God gently reminds us that He is ever-present.

After recovering from her volatile relationship and vowing to be content being single, Keisa met the love of her life. While living in bliss, tragedy struck in the most devastating way. Her husband was killed in a car accident on his way home from work. Kesia, now a young widow, was down to her very last dime. She had spent her last five dollars on gas. Her rent was due and her baby needed milk and pampers.

"Where are You?" Kesia began to cry out, reminding God that He was her Provider and that she needed Him to supply all that she needed. Her eyes filled with tears. She could not see where her situation would ever change. She felt God was punishing her. She asked, "Why me? What did I do to deserve this?"

God had allowed her husband to be taken away from her, and she struggled financially. She wanted to give up. She frequently thought about ending her life, but she knew her baby had no one else. Then a song came on the radio about God's provision for His people. She went to sleep listening to the song all night. When she got to work the next day, an older co-worker told Kesia that she was heavy in her spirit the night before and that God instructed her to bless her. She gave her a check for one thousand dollars. Kesia had asked and cried out, and God showed up right on time. She fell to her knees and begin to thank Him for being on time and supplying her needs. He is always on time!

APPLICATION

God sends reminders throughout the day of His spirit that is working within you. Being in position is the key. The way to start identifying those reminders and His spirit working within is by practicing being present with Him. Practice meditating and being open and available. It is through your demeanor and disposition that allow you to become open enough to be able to see Him at work in your life. The more time you spend with Him, the more you connect with Him in an unbelievable way.

It is God's will for us not to suffer, lack, or need anything. God shall supply all of your needs according to his riches in glory. God is omnipresent, present everywhere. God is beyond us. We cannot begin to understand how He is all knowing and has all power is in His hands. He is always near to us. He makes Himself known to those who call on Him, serve Him, seek Him, worship Him, praise Him, and pray to Him. All God needs is a willing vessel.

PRAYER

Father, thank You for being all knowing and having all power. Thank You for never leaving nor forsaking me. Thank You that You know my fears, needs, and secrets. Yet, You still graciously love me. I celebrate Your timing. I am forever thankful, forever grateful, and always available to You. Amen.

DAY 4

WISDOM PRODUCES FAITH

Can we trust in the Lord at all times?

"Trust in the LORD with all thine heart; and lean not unto thine own understanding."

(PROVERBS 3:5)

STORY

Faith is believing without a shadow of a doubt that God is God and that He has all power in His hands. He will do what He said He would do.

After watching the drunk driver that killed her husband walk away free, a spark for

justice ignited in Kesia and she decided to go back to school. While a college student, she was also a widow, on her own with a child. She was at the end of her rope. It was her senior year and last semester of college. Kesia worked two jobs to put herself through college. She was determined to graduate. Unfortunately, she received a notice from the Financial Aid Office stating she would not be eligible to graduate because her financial aid funding had run out. Kesia was barely making ends meet as it was. She felt her dream of becoming a federal investigator was over.

Her grandmother told her when she was a child to always trust in the Lord and that if she had faith the size of a mustard seed, she could speak to the situation. Kesia was told to always talk to God and to trust His timing. Remembering her grandmother's words, she told God that she did not believe He would have brought her as far as He had to leave her. She began to pray. She prayed all night and she woke up with a spirit of peace. She began to thank and praise God in advance for answering her prayers. She reflected back on the talks she had with her grandma. She could hear her grandma say, "God will make a way, trust Him!"

The phone rang and it was the Financial Aid Office calling to say there has been a mistake. Her account was paid in full! In that moment, she realized that God's timing is always on time, and that He only wants the best for her.

APPLICATION

Wisdom is a learning process each day. It requires developing a relationship with God. To receive wisdom from God, you must ask faithfully in His name. You must be God-fearing, humble, peaceful, and considerate. Wisdom comes from seeking God in prayer and reading His word. It comes from spending alone time with God and listening for His still small voice. Make an intentional decision to trust God and allow Him to guide your thoughts. Honor His word and practice discipline. You must take every opportunity possible to saturate your heart and mind with God's word. One of the most powerful things you can do is replace negative thoughts and feelings with Gods promises. It requires listening to God's instruction and not others' or your own. Having faithful, honest, and caring believers in our lives to help hold us to a higher standard and hold us accountable so we do not fall short is important. Wisdom is the ability to choose right over wrong, compassion over resentment, and unbiasedness over judgment. When you follow God's instructions, you earn favor with God.

PRAYER

Sovereign God, how excellent is Your name in all the earth. You are awesome, majestic, marvelous, miraculous, and perfect in all of Your ways. You know my name, and I praise You for who You are to me. In Jesus' name, Amen.

DAY 5

WISDOM PRODUCES PEACE

Why do we give people power?

"So that your faith might not rest in wisdom of men but in the power of God."
(I CORINTHIANS 2:5, ESV)

STORY

What happens when the world encourages people to get more degrees to get the more money? The higher the degree, the higher the position. This mindset has become the driving force of many in the world. This mindset can lead to envy, jealousy, and destruction.

Kesia, considered herself as a self-made survivor who could accomplish anything. Her now well-known status and social-driven success caused her care more about others' opinions than God's. She felt that the only way to get ahead was to manipulate situations, circumstances, and people. She felt that status defined who she was. She falsely qualified for positions. She always made sure she was the center of attention.

Why was this so? Was it because in society titles lead to entitlement and power and jobs, positions and titles to override qualifications and dedication? Is this because the world has given power to man? Unfortunately, the wrong message is being sent about education and the workplace. People are forgetting that only what is done from the heart will last.

It is time to stop giving people so much power over you. God is your source and strength. God is the one who creates positions, companies, and titles. If God used Moses who was not eloquent in speech and afraid to lead God's people, the Hebrews, out of bondage in Egypt and into the promised land of Canaan, He will create a position just for you. It is time to seek God's direction and will for your life. When positions are given to people based on integrity, values and dedication, there will be peace, harmony, and success in the work place. God is the only one who gives promotion, not man.

APPLICATION

Ask God daily to search the hearts of people and reveal their motives. Take God's word and apply it to every aspect of your life.

Moses was a prophet and a leader. He was also a murderer. Yet, God still saw fit to use him and make his name great. Moses had to overcome fear and trust God's plan and will for his life. He applied his faith over fear. He surrendered his will to God's will. Moses' faith, trust, and obedience to God allowed him to be used in a mighty way by God. God opened doors, fought battles, and kept him safe.

God is not respecter of person, and He will right the wrongs. Stop putting your trust in man because what God has for you is for you. Whatever God's plans are for you will always trump man's plans. God has the power to open and close doors. Wisdom along with knowledge will help you to know God intimately. Knowing God's heart helps us to make life choices and deepens our sense of humanity.

PRAYER

Gracious Father, thank You for being the author and finisher of my faith. I rejoice because You have the final say. Thank You for the plans You have to prosper me and not fail me. Thank You for the many blessings with my name on them. Thank You for making crooked places straight. My hope is in You. Amen.

JULY
WEEK 6

DAY 1
THE PAIN OF HURT

How deep is your hurt?

"In the multitude of words there wanteth not sin: but he that refraineth his lips is wise."
(PROVERBS 10:19)

STORY

"You think you know it all! That's why no one wants to be around you!" Lynette shouted.

Taylor could not believe the words coming out of her sister's mouth. She looked at Lynette as if she had three heads and each was speaking in a foreign language. How did a simple discussion to plan their annual sister trip escalate to this?

They had not agreed on a location or expenses, but Taylor could not believe her sister would say that to her. Who didn't want to be around her? Was this how Lynette felt, and she was just adding others to give validity to her opinion? Taylor's mind raced and questioned every encounter they had recently.

The pain Taylor felt was wrenching. She felt anger and hurt simultaneously. The urge to cry was intense, but she refused to let Lynette see her cry. She got up, grabbed her purse, and walked out of the door. She held back the tears until she got to her car. Taylor could not understand why Lynette was spewing venom, but she was not going to allow her another chance. When her phone rang, and Taylor saw it was Lynette calling, she immediately hit decline. Talking to her sister was the last thing she wanted to do.

APPLICATION

It is not uncommon to find yourself in situations where you disagree with others. Differences of opinion are a normal part of life. How you respond in those situations is important. Discussion and debate can be healthy and bring clarity. Lively debate can even be a good thing. When conversations and dialogue move from helpful to hurtful, lines are crossed and communication breaks down, even deteriorates.

Someone once said, "Least said, soonest mended." Be careful of the words you choose because the harm they cause can be irreparable. Words are powerful and can bring encouragement or discouragement, be helpful or a hindrance. Before you speak, consider the impact your words will have. Will they heal or hurt? Is your intention to do damage that cannot be undone? Carefully choose your words. Even if you are angry, pause before you say something you will regret. Would you embrace the words you have spoken if the roles reversed and the same words were said to you?

Many people think "I'm sorry" will take care of everything. They believe that it does not matter what you do or say, "I'm sorry" will reverse it all. You should understand that those words do not undo the damage caused by negative communication. Words can be like nails in a board. You may pull out the nail, but the hole is still left behind. Before you unleash a tornado of words, carefully consider the good or bad results that will result from them.

PRAYER

Heavenly Father, please help me to remember the power of my words. Help me to build up and not tear down others with my communication. May my words and attitude be pleasing unto You. If my words will destroy, help me to reconsider them before they leave my mouth. Let the words that I speak be edifying. If I get angry, help me not to sin and leave devastation behind when I respond. Help me to be quick to hear, slow to speak, and slow to anger. Bridle my tongue so that I do not ruin a relationship or break someone's spirit with my words. May You be proud of me and all of my interactions. Give me a clean heart and help me to follow You. In Jesus' precious name, Amen.

DAY 2

THE WEIGHT OF UNFORGIVENESS

How heavy is the load you are carrying?

"But if ye forgive not men their trespasses, neither will your Father forgive your trespasses."

(MATTHEW 6:15)

STORY

It had been an emotional few months for Taylor. She and her best friend Janelle were having lunch to catch up and unwind.

Janelle asked, "Have you talked to your sister yet?"

Taylor looked at her as if she had totally lost her mind, and she was not in the mood to help her find it.

108

"I don't have anything to say to her, and I don't want to hear anything she has to say to me."

Taylor had not spoken to Lynette in months since the disagreement about the annual trip. Taylor had always been the one to take the high road, to keep the peace in the family, but not this time. Janelle reminded Taylor about turning the other cheek. Taylor had another cheek in mind.

Every time Taylor thought about their encounter, she got angry, but more than anything, she was hurt. She reflected back on all their interactions over the years. Lynette was the older sister, but she was not a nice person. Taylor loved her anyway, but this time, she had gone too far.

Janelle saw the tears in Taylor's eyes. She hugged her tightly and whispered, "Let it go, Taylor. Forgiveness is for you, not her."

APPLICATION

We all can recall someone who has hurt our feelings. When we were children, we may have been hurt by another child who did not want to play with us, made fun of us, or denied us when others were around. We may have been hurt by a sibling who teased us, made us cry, or made us so angry that we made them cry. As we grew older, the hurts changed. The opportunities to hurt and be hurt increased as we navigated and developed relationships. The more important the person was to us, the more susceptible we were to being hurt. The stronger the bond, the bigger the hurt. Sometimes, "I'm sorry" was usually all that was needed to forgive the affront. Some wounds heal quickly. We forgive and forget. We move on until the next time. However, sometimes the forgiveness does not come as easily. The hurt can be too deep and the cause of it unforgiven!

Not practicing forgiveness weighs us down emotionally. We wrap the pain we experienced around us like a blanket. We use it to protect ourselves and keep others at a distance, but we are hurting ourselves. Not forgiving others affects us, even if we do not realize it or are not willing to admit it. We internalize the hurt while our offenders go on with their lives, unaware or uncaring about the damage they have caused. God commands us to forgive. Forgiveness is so important that He declares that if we **do not** forgive, we **will not** be forgiven. Forgiveness frees us from the past and allows us to lose the weight of not forgiving others.

PRAYER

Heavenly Father, sometimes I feel helpless. I admit to being angry and hurt and not being able to get past it. When I feel wronged, I just want to protect myself and keep those that hurt me at bay. Help me to forgive even when I do not want to. Whether someone hurt me intentionally or accidentally, the pain is still there. I realize that I cannot forgive on my own and need Your help. With Your help, I can truly let go and let You have Your way in my life. Search my heart, and if You find anything displeasing to You, please remove it. I am grateful that You continue to forgive me of my sins and mistakes. Help me to show the same grace to others. Let Your love shine through me. In Jesus' precious name I pray, Amen.

DAY 3

THE SILENCE IS DEAFENING

How can you hear if you are not listening?

"Be still, and know that I am God: I will be exalted among the heathen, I will be exalted in the earth."
(PSALM 46:10)

STORY

Taylor was glad to see 5 p.m. finally arrive. Her days were filled with meetings and more meetings. She had worked late every night the past few weeks to bring the project in on time and on budget. It was wearing her down. She rubbed the back of her neck, feeling exhausted. She refused to take work home this weekend. She needed a break from the routine. Taylor checked her calendar one last time to verify next week's schedule. She noticed that an additional late afternoon meeting had been added. She sighed heavily as she shut down her computer. She asked God to deliver her from the stress before pushing away from her desk.

Taylor realized she could not continue at this pace. Long days, late nights, and little sleep was a poor combination. Each time she spoke to her director, she was assured that they were looking to hire an assistant to help alleviate her workload. Taylor felt her reward for doing a good job was more work. Something had to give. She had prayed for direction, but so far, God had been silent. Maybe she should consider one of the headhunter's offers she had received.

Taylor said, "Lord, I need you now!"

APPLICATION

Sometimes, we get so busy in life that we are busy being busy. We navigate from one task to the next, one project to another. We toss in events and our families for good measure. The juggling act can be overwhelming. Trying to keep all of the balls in the air can tax the most organized person. If our busyness has a lot of overlap, we can come undone. We realize that our full plates have become platters. We pray for guidance, even clarity in between it all. We want a fast answer. We expect God to work it out for our good and cover us in the storm. Yet, we continue the momentum, not slowing down.

Our world is fast-paced, and we want God to keep up with us. We forget that it is His lead we should follow. God's timing is not our timing. His timing is always perfect. The same God that delivered the Israelites safely is the same God who is watching over us. When we cannot see what is ahead, we need to look back and remind ourselves of His record of accomplishment. Every victory was because of God. Every mountain climbed was with His guidance. Even in the valleys, He was there.

God's word reminds us to lean not on our own understanding. God desires our attention. He is a jealous God who does not want to share our focus with everything else. He wants to be our priority and first thought, not an afterthought. When we ask God a question, we must stop to listen for the answer.

PRAYER

Heavenly Father, thank You for hearing me when I call. I feel so overwhelmed and do not know what to do. Father, help me to trust in You when I feel like I am being drenched by the storm. I know You will cover me. Help me to rest in the safety of Your arms. Forgive me for not being faithful in my devotional time, for prioritizing anything before You. I realize everything I have and ever will have is because of Your grace. Help me not to take anything for granted. Father, help me to dialogue with You, not just perform a monologue. When I rise in the morning, be my first thought, and be my last thought as I close my eyes at night. Help me to be still and block out the noise of the world to hear Your voice. Speak Lord. I am listening. Amen.

DAY 4

THE POSSIBILITIES ARE ENDLESS

What if failure was not an option?

"I can do all things through Christ which strengtheneth me."
(PHILIPPIANS 4:13)

STORY

"I got the offer!" Taylor yelled excitedly as soon as Janelle answered the phone.

"Congratulations!" Janelle yelled back. "You've been waiting for this for a while."

Taylor nodded her head in agreement. It had been almost a year since she began the process.

At one point, she was not sure that she wanted to continue. Doubt crept in several times. Could she do it? Did she have the skillset to be successful? Despite the Senior Director position being a great opportunity, it was in another city and state. What if she got there and did not like the people or they did not like her?

Each time uncertainty reared its head, she reached out to Janelle. Together they would pray and she could feel God's presence. Janelle would remind her that God would finish the good work He had begun in her life.

Taylor had worked toward this her entire career. Sometimes she had taken positions paying less to gain the experience needed. She did not want to uproot her entire life, but she remembered that every path God had laid before her took her to the destination He desired. This would be no different. She was trusting God to be with her every step of the way.

APPLICATION

"What do you want to be when you grow up?" Most of us can recall being asked this question as a child. At family gatherings, church events, or at school functions, some adult would invariably pop the question. With a child's limitless imagination, we fantasized about the endless possibilities of being grown. We observed the adults around us and daydreamed of following in their footsteps.

We read books and watched television, inserting ourselves in the place of the characters on the pages and screens. We dared to dream, and the possibilities were endless. We dreamed of becoming doctors, lawyers, teachers, models, actors, or professional athletes. Some of us just wanted to be famous, it did not matter what we had to do to get there. When we did not pass our dreams through a filter to sift out what others believed to be unachievable, we believed we could become anything our hearts desired. Sometimes we held true to those childhood fantasies, and other times, dream killers popped our balloons or life caused a detour.

In Jeremiah, God told the exiles not to believe the false reports. He had plans to prosper them and not to harm them, to give them a hope and a future. God has not changed. He is the same now as He was then. He wants the best for us. We have to be willing to do the work, to press on in spite of the circumstances. The race will be won, if we endure. He promised to be with us every step of the way.

PRAYER

Heavenly Father, I know that You will supply all of my needs. You have opened doors for me that I was not always qualified to enter. When I look back at my life, I can see Your hand of guidance. When I obeyed and followed Your lead, things turned out well. When I went off on my own, thinking I knew better, I ended up in a mess. Then, I looked to You to fix it. Help me to remember that it is You who orders my steps. When I cannot see my way, Father, shine a light on the path I should take. Give me wisdom to know the difference between what is meant for me and what I should avoid. In Jesus' name, Amen.

DAY 5

THE NEW NORMAL BEGINS

How can you mend a broken heart?

*"He healeth the broken in heart,
and bindeth up their wounds."*
(PSALM 147:3)

STORY

Taylor pressed the button to end the call. A sob caught in her throat as she realized what she had done. Habitually, she had again tried to call her Mom to share some news. Unfortunately, that was no longer possible. She looked at the calendar. It was six months to the day since her mom had died. Maybe she should delete her number, but she was not ready for that final act. She still could not quite believe that she was gone.

Taylor glanced at the family portrait on her desk. It was taken the last time she and her siblings were together, before her mom got sick. The smiles were evidence that no one had the slightest clue of the darkness that was lurking inside her mom's body. It unleashed a nightmare from which Taylor still had not awakened. Cancer stole her mom. It ravaged her body and cruelly took everything that was vibrant about her. The carnage left behind was a hole in Taylor's heart and their family unit. The pain at times was so unbearable that it felt as if it would overtake her. People kept saying, "Time heals all wounds." Taylor wished someone would fast-forward the clock so the grief she was experiencing would not last as long.

APPLICATION

The pain of losing a loved one can be debilitating. Being told an illness will end in death does not necessarily diminish the pain when death actually claims our loved one. We think we can prepare ourselves and brace for the inevitable, but until death comes, everything is theoretical, pending. You never really know how you will act or feel until reality hits.

The Bible says to be absent from the body is to be present with the Lord. People like to tell us that our loved one is in a better place. While our heads know this, our hearts still feel the pain. The rawness and intensity of the pain can fade with time. It changes and is not as prevalent. It is not gone; it is just not right on the surface.

It is important that we allow ourselves time to grieve. We must keep in mind that the time needed varies from person to person. Although we may desire instant relief, we must take the steps toward healing. There is not an established timeframe for grief to end. Sometimes, a single word, a scent, or a picture vividly reminds us of our transitioned loved one and takes us back to the beginning of the pain. When this happens, we need to reset and continue. We must remember the promises of God and trust that He will see us through. We are not to grieve as if we do not have hope. God promises to be with us and to wipe away all of our tears.

PRAYER

Heavenly Father, You are all seeing and all knowing. You see behind the mask that I wear daily to exhibit strength to the world. I project the image others want to see because no one really wants to know the real answer when they ask if I am okay. It is the polite thing to ask, but if the response is anything other than positive, they are uncomfortable. Therefore, I bind up my emotions to avoid being overwhelmed. It feels like a flood is raging within me. Inside I am crumbling. I push myself to exhaustion so that there is no time to focus on my pain. If I am too tired to think, I am too tired to feel. Avoidance is easier than acknowledging the loss. This has become a vicious cycle, and I need Your help. Help them to see me. Help me to let them. In Jesus' name, Amen.

JULY
WEEK 7

DAY 1
THE LOVE

Do you know that He loves you?

"Charity suffereth long, and is kind; charity envieth not; charity vaunteth not itself, is not puffed up, Doth not behave itself unseemly, seeketh not her own, is not easily provoked, thinketh no evil; Rejoiceth not in iniquity, but rejoiceth in the truth; Beareth all things, believeth all things, hopeth all things, endureth all things. Charity never faileth: but whether there be prophecies, they shall fail; whether there be tongues, they shall cease; whether there be knowledge, it shall vanish away."

(I CORINTHIANS 13:4-8)

STORY

As Shaivon drove down the expressway to her fourth job interview, she could not stop thinking about how she would answer the questions asked of her. The entire time she was

riding to her destination, she was praying for guidance. After all, this was her fourth interview. As she drove, she continued to review the interview answers in her head, repeatedly.

After driving for about thirty minutes, Shaivon finally arrived at the elementary school. She pulled into the parking space and realized that she had about twenty minutes before her interview began. Because she had some extra time, she pulled out a stack of papers with possible interview questions. As she sat in the car, she reviewed the questions and answered them aloud. With ten minutes left, she got out of the car and began to walk to the school building.

Once she entered the school, she approached the front office. Shaivon checked in with the secretary who asked her to have a seat. After about five minutes, she was greeted by the principal and asked to enter the conference room for the interview. She met with a panel of five people. The interview lasted about twenty-five minutes. After the interview was over, Shaivon left the conference room confident that she had the job. She got in her car and shouted, "I got this."

Two weeks later, she discovered that she was not the winning candidate.

APPLICATION

Each day we face difficulties. Some doors are opened for us and some are closed. Even when we are overly prepared and think that we have it all together, things do not always go our way. Our way is often not God's way. God's plan is bigger than our plan.

When you feel that God is not answering your prayers, count it all joy! Count it all joy even when God closes the door on your plan. Trust and be patient because God has your back. Stay the course and remain patient. God will plant you where He wants you to be rooted and grounded for growth in His spirit.

PRAYER

Father God who art in heaven, I know that Your plans are bigger than my plans. Father, please show me where You would like me to be. Lord, I submit to Your way, and I will continue to prepare myself for the job that You choose as my blessing. Please align my plan with Your plan. I will wait patiently for my seed to be planted on fertile ground. I know that You love me and will take care of my every need. I thank You in advance for all that You do. In Jesus' name, Amen.

DAY 2
THE TEACHING

How patient are you?

"Preach the word; be instant in season, out of season; reprove, rebuke, exhort with all long suffering and doctrine."
(II TIMOTHY 4:2)

STORY

Disappointed, Shaivon continued to pray that she would land her desired job. Soon after, she received a phone call from a middle school. The assistant principal asked her to come in for an interview. This would be Shaivon's fifth interview. Nervous and hopeful at the same time, Shaivon entered the middle school for her interview. She met with an interview panel of three. After the interview was complete, she walked away with the feeling her prayer, preparation, and practice from her four previous interviews had paid off. Shaivon left feeling as if God had taken control. She was correct! She got the job!

APPLICATION

Have you ever felt like you have been dedicated to God's way but that your requests are not being heard? Remember, His time is not your time. Just know that God loves you and will provide you with all of your needs in due season. What looks like suffering to us is merely training in God's sight. He will use your preparation and practice as building blocks for the next level. Be patient and trust God's plan for you!

PRAYER

Father God that art in heaven, I know that Your plans are bigger than my plans. Father God, I thank You for the position where You have placed me. I thank You for allowing me to use my time to prepare and practice. I thank You for teaching me how to be patient. Continue to lead and guide me as I do Your mighty work. I thank You in advance for all that You do and will continue to do. In Jesus' name, Amen.

DAY 3
THE WORK

Are you willing to put in the work?

"But let patience have her perfect work, that ye may be perfect and entire, wanting nothing. If any of you lack wisdom, let him ask of God, that giveth to all men liberally, and upbraideth not; and it shall be given him. But let him ask in faith, nothing wavering. For he that wavereth is like a wave of the sea driven with the wind and tossed. For let not that man think that he shall receive any thing of the Lord."

(JAMES 1:4-7)

STORY

Shaivon gave God all of the praise for opening a new door for her. All of her prayers, labor, and groundwork had paid off. This job began an exciting new chapter in her life. Shaivon had graciously transitioned from being a middle school classroom teacher to becoming a middle school counselor. She would continue to use her God-given gifts to inspire, encourage, and support students, but now she would do this at the middle school level. At least that is what Shaivon thought.

After working in her new position, meeting new people, and learning new skills, Shaivon and the other two counselors were called into the principal's office. The three of them were informed that because a new school was opening, one of them would have to volunteer to go to the new school. All three of the counselors were adamant about not wanting to leave. Shaivon, especially, was not going to volunteer because, after all, she had just gotten there.

Shaivon, asked, "What if no one volunteers?"

The principal looked at Shaivon and said, "If none of you volunteer, then you will have to go."

Shaivon was stunned. "Why me?" she asked.

The principal stated, "Because you were the last one hired."

APPLICATION

What is patience? Patience is the ability to wait without becoming angry. Think of a time when you patiently prayed and fasted for a breakthrough, and you got it, only to find out that life would soon throw you a curve ball. You see, we cannot predict the future. Only God knows what lies ahead. You should rethink, recharge, and reconnect with God. He has gone before you and has planned that path that you will take. Remain patient and trust His guidance and plans for where He is taking you next.

PRAYER

Father God who art in heaven, thank You for being a just God. Thank You for being a faithful, God. Thank You for placing each steppingstone in just the right place, in accordance with Your will. Because of Your greatness, I know that each step that I take will be covered. I trust You, Lord. In Jesus' name, Amen.

DAY 4

THE STRENGTH

Can you endure until the end?

*"Wait on the LORD: be of good courage,
and he shall strengthen thine heart:
wait, I say, on the LORD."*
(PSALM 27:14)

STORY

Shaivon was stunned when she heard the disappointing news about the possibility of having to leave the new job that she had just started. Feelings of confusion and frustration set in. Shaivon could not understand why God would bless her with a new job, simply to move her after one year. All of this would be against

her will. At the end of the day, Shaivon felt that she had no control over her destiny. The decision sat on the shoulders of her co-counselors or so Shaivon thought.

As the end of the school year approached, the principal called Shaivon into his office. He told her that since no one volunteered from the counseling department to go to the new school, she would be required to transfer. As Shaivon walked out of the office, she prayed and asked God to give her the strength to endure until the end. Immediately, He turned her frustrating thoughts into pleasant thoughts of working at the brand-new school.

APPLICATION

What message was God sending Shaivon? When you feel that God has changed your path, the message is to stay committed. God wants to know that you can endure through the season that He has set before you. Stay the course, even when life seems impossible and uncomfortable. Dig deep and finish strong!

PRAYER

Father God who art in heaven, thank You for giving me the strength to endure through my ups and my downs. I thank You for setting my path straight, even when I wanted to turn around. Thank You for closing one door and opening a new door. I look forward to what You have in store for my future. Thank You, God, for being my rock. In Jesus' name, Amen.

DAY 5

THE DELIVERANCE

Do you know that He can deliver you?

*"I waited patiently for the LORD; and he inclined
unto me, and heard my cry. He brought me up also
out of an horrible pit, out of the miry clay, and set
my feet upon a rock, and established my goings.
And he hath put a new song in my mouth, even
praise unto our God: many shall see it, and fear,
and shall trust in the LORD."*

(*PSALM 40:1-3*)

STORY

As Shaivon drove to the new school, she
had lots of time to envision the new
adventure God had set before her. She had
many thoughts that were positive benefits
of being at the new school. Shaivon realized

that the principal was God-fearing and family oriented. Her commute was cut in half, and she did not have to share an office. She had her own. It was a bittersweet shift. She could have never dreamed a situation possible. She finally saw God's plan. God delivered her from a decent position to an exemplary position. He made her the last hired, so that she could be the first promoted. As Shaivon drove onto the campus of the new school, she sung praises of thanksgiving unto the Lord.

APPLICATION

Has God ever set you up so that you could see His power? Did you think of all the wonderful benefits that came along with His setup? God's path is your path when you live your life according to His word. Stay committed, even through your long-suffering. Stay committed, even when you are confused. Trust that God has your back. He will take care of all of your needs. He will deliver you!

PRAYER

Father God that art in heaven, thank You for promoting me to a place that honors You. Your deliverance has set me free. I know that it is only by Your grace and mercy that I receive blessings from You. I love You dearly, and I humbly ask that You continue to keep me and never forsake me. You are wonderful, and my heart is forever grateful to You. Praises unto You! In Jesus' name, I pray, Amen.

JULY
WEEK 8

DAY 1
GETTING STRAIGHT

What is it that you truly believe?

*"He that walketh uprightly walketh surely:
but he that perverteth his ways shall be known."*
(PROVERBS 10:9)

STORY

Kyle worked for a production company in Los Angeles. She was raised in the church, but when she went away to college, she just did not get around to getting up on Sundays to go to chapel. The next thing she knew, four years had passed since she had set foot in a church.

Right after she finished college, her parents died. She and her siblings did not get along, so she had been truly alone, trying to navigate as an adult. Life was hard for her. She had no use for the Christian message that Jesus is the answer for everything. She did not feel as though Jesus had been her answer or shown up when she had troubles. She believed that she would figure everything out for herself. In her mind, she did not need Jesus to save her.

Kyle believed in God but viewed Him as passive, watching us from a distance. She was not so sure about the Jesus part. She believed the Bible was mostly true, although she'd never really read it, but she thought that some of what it said was outdated, particularly the part about not having sex outside of marriage. Kyle told one of her friends that it just was not realistic in this day and age to think that you can date someone for very long without being physically intimate.

Although Kyle believed she was a Christian, she did not talk much about that around her LA friends. It was just not a good look to be a Christian in Hollywood. If people knew you were a Christian, they began asking you a lot of questions like "Do you think homosexuality is a sin?" If you answer that question the wrong way, you will never work again in that town. Kyle was not denying that she was a Christian; she was just not making it known.

APPLICATION

In order to know truth, we have to hear truth. In order to hear truth, we have to open up our hearts to it. The Bible talks many times about hardening one's heart. That means being closed off to the truth and not wanting to hear it. Often times, someone can be speaking truth in our lives, whether it be in conversation or from the pulpit, and we reject it.

Kyle did not know truth because she had prejudged what truth was. She believed that the Bible was the word of God, but she was not sure that she believed all of what it said. She had her own thoughts about life, but her ideas were all over the place and had been influenced by what was popular and politically correct. She had cherry-picked the Bible.

Having integrity means, in part, that we are seekers of the truth and that we want to hear what is right and what is just. If we have integrity, we do not simply accept the politically correct norm of the day when it contradicts God's word. Integrity means that your heart and your mind are one in truth. Kyle was struggling not only with what she believed, but also with also with who she believed, God or the world.

PRAYER

Father God, I come in the name of Jesus and ask You to forgive me of my sins. I ask that You cleanse me and make me a new creature in Christ Jesus. I ask, Lord, that You would set me free from all unrighteousness and that You would give me clean hands and a pure heart. Lord, I want to know You better. Create in me a clean heart and renew a right spirit within me. Cast me not away from Your presence and do not take Your Holy Spirit from me. Lord, let me be a woman of truth and woman of faith. Let me speak boldly on Your behalf as an ambassador of Christ Jesus. In Jesus' holy name, I pray, Amen.

SPEAKING LOVE

Do you desire blessings or curses?

"The integrity of the upright shall guide them: but the perverseness of transgressors shall destroy them."
(PROVERBS 11:3)

STORY

One night, Kyle's best friend Courtney called in a panic. She was getting married in a month and had gone out drinking with some friends to celebrate. She got so drunk that she did not remember the night at all. Courtney's friend Rhonda told her that she had been making out with one of the guys. She could not believe what had she done. She was so ashamed.

She loved her fiancé, John. She told Kyle that she was never going to drink again.

That juicy bit of gossip was too good to hold. Immediately, Kyle was on the phone with girlfriend after girlfriend laughing about what Courtney had done. The next day, Courtney herself was laughing because Rhonda was just trying to teach her a lesson. Nothing had happened the night before except that Courtney had been drunk and passed out. Courtney decided to keep her vow to never to drink again.

The following week, Kyle heard that Courtney and John had broken up and were not getting married. She wondered why she had not heard it directly from Courtney. She called Courtney repeatedly, but there was no answer. Finally, Rhonda called and said that Courtney never wanted to speak to Kyle again. John had broken up with Courtney after he heard the gossip that Kyle had spread.

APPLICATION

With one careless act, Kyle destroyed a lifelong friendship and brought destruction to someone else's life. Gossip is a selfish and perverse sin. It causes us to laugh about other's misery and rejoice in their downfalls. Courtney trusted Kyle with her shame, but Kyle was not a trustworthy friend. She did not keep the confidence. She was two-faced and a fraud. She showed herself to be sympathetic to Courtney's situation, but then treacherously laughed at her pain behind her back. She was more interested in the momentary pleasure she got from passing on a good story than the deep regret that her friend was experiencing.

Do these words seem harsh? If so, is it because it is common for us to all dabble in a little gossip here and there? That is the way of the world. Gossip is something evil that will bring ruin to gossipers because it hardens our hearts to the struggles and pains of other people and causes us to find pleasure in them. As we sin against our sister or brother, we ruin our own character and lose favor with God.

Be careful because gossip is addictive. The more you do it, the easier it becomes to gossip even more. The opposite is also true. The more we are selfless and honor other people, the easier it becomes to be their true friend and a blessing to them.

PRAYER

Father God, I come in the name of Jesus. I pray that nothing unclean comes from my lips. I pray that the enemy would have no victory through my tongue. I pray, Lord, that I will not deceive myself by my mouth. Lord, I pray that when I speak, I would speak only what my Father has taught me to say through Jesus Christ, my Lord. Let there be no judgment or criticism that is uttered from my heart, but instead, let my words be full of blessings for myself and others. It is my desire always to lift my voice to You, oh God, with praise and thanksgiving. I pray in the name of Jesus Christ, my Lord, Amen.

DAY 3

PLEASING GOD

Are you willing to let God transform you?

"I know also, my God, that thou triest the heart, and hast pleasure in uprightness. As for me, in the uprightness of mine heart I have willingly offered all these things: and now have I seen with joy thy people, which are present here, to offer willingly unto thee."

(I CHRONICLES 29:17)

STORY

At first, Kyle was defensive about her gossiping being the cause of Courtney and John breaking up. The first thing out of her mouth was that Courtney should not have been out that night, and she certainly should not have gotten drunk. Who knows? Maybe she was

messing around with another guy. It could have happened. Maybe she told someone else. Maybe the gossip did not originate with her. After all, Rhonda knew as well. Maybe she was the one spread the story around.

Finally, Kyle was so miserable about the rift with her lifelong friend that she admitted to herself that she messed up. But now what? Why couldn't Courtney just forgive her so they could be friends like before?

It was almost a year later that Kyle heard that Courtney and John had reunited and were getting married. This time, Courtney did not ask Kyle to be her maid of honor. She was not even invited to the wedding. Kyle had reached her breaking point, but in her heart, she knew that she had brought all this pain on herself. She turned on the TV to her favorite gossip show, and all of a sudden, it was not fun anymore. As she flipped the channels, she stopped on a channel where a pastor was preaching. She said, "Are you willing to let God transform you?"

In a small quiet voice, Kyle whispered, "Yes."

APPLICATION

Just as with one careless act, Kyle gave victory to sin, with one intentional whisper, God brought victory to her life for eternity. She had lost so much—her parents, her siblings, her best friend, and most of her other friends who had abandoned her because of what she had done to Courtney. She did not want to keep losing in life. She wanted to be different. She not only wanted to say she was sorry, but she wanted to walk in repentance of this sin and all of her sins. God was right there.

He was ready to transform her and ready to give her a new name. He was ready and waiting to be pleased with her.

God stands at the door and invites each one of us in. If we are willing to give Him our hearts, He is willing to give us His. God looks for these pure moments in us, moments when we are the most vulnerable and moments when we have no other motive than to surrender ourselves to Him. These are the tender moments in which God knows that our offering is brought without hypocrisy, but simply to glorify Him.

Although born out of a broken heart, the most glorious thing happened to Kyle in that moment. With that whisper, she turned her heart toward God. We can each do the same; we can come before the God of the universe and give Him the pureness of our hearts.

P R A Y E R

Father God, I thank You that You never give up on me. I thank You that You never stop chasing me. I thank You that You will never turn me away if I seek Your face. I thank You that if I seek You, I will find You because it is Your desire that I not perish but know Your saving grace. I thank You that You leave the ninety-nine to go after the one. I thank You, Lord, that as much as I mess up and as much as I am a mess, You can mold me into something better than this. You can give me hope and a future. Thank You. In the name of Jesus, Amen.

DAY 4
HEALING HURTS

Can you stand upright?

"The sacrifices of God are a broken spirit:
a broken and a contrite heart,
O God, thou wilt not despise."
(PSALM 51:17)

STORY

Kyle was broken. She did not know who she was anymore. She certainly was not the kind and loving person she thought she was. When she looked in the mirror now, she only saw a selfish, self-centered person who lived just for herself. For the first time in her life, she realized that she was not in control and that there was someone bigger than her, someone she had been fighting against her whole life. She had been fighting against God, the one who wanted nothing more than to give her life.

Right there in front of the TV evangelist whom God had used to call her closer to Him, Kyle gave her life to Jesus. She made Him ruler of her life and surrendered it all. She fell on her knees and sobbed for hours, letting out all of the pain and anguish of her own life. She cried out to God about the loss of her parents, her siblings, and her friends. She cried until she could not cry anymore. She was exhausted, but a sense of relief and a peace she had never known before came over her. She felt as if she were being rocked in the arms of Jesus as she drifted into sleep.

APPLICATION

Kyle was full of pain and anguish, not just because she had lost a friend and everyone seemed to know what she had done, but because she was forced to face the darkness of her own heart. She was a broken woman because God could not use her until she was broken. She had to be broken of pride, selfishness, and evil. Now, the door was open for her to be transformed into the woman of God that she was created to be.

Becoming a woman of God is a process. Like a young child who has to crawl before she walks, it will take a minute before you can stand upright in His presence. First, you have to release all of the muck and mire that you have been carrying around with you as if it were valuable when, in fact, it was weighing you down.

Like Kyle, we may fall contrite before the Lord and cry until we cannot cry anymore. Such a cry is not just a ball your eyes out cry where the problem is still there when we finish crying. On the other side of this snotty cry, there is hope, light, and life. Jesus is on the other side with His arms open wide, ready to embrace you as a daughter of the Most High God.

PRAYER

Dear God, I thank You for hearing my cry and soothing my soul. Though the process was painful, being broken led me into Your arms and revealed to me just how much I need You. I will follow You all the days of my life. Because of You, I can stand upright. You have healed the hurt that caused me pain. You have brought me closer to You. I will dwell forever in Your arms. In Jesus' name I pray, Amen.

DAY 5
KEEPING COOL

Is Jesus enough for you?

"And the LORD said unto Satan, Hast thou considered my servant Job, that there is none like him in the earth, a perfect and an upright man, one that feareth God, and escheweth evil? and still he holdeth fast his integrity, although thou movedst me against him, to destroy him without cause."

(JOB 2:3)

STORY

The next day on her way to work, Kyle walked to the other side of the street when she saw the old man on the corner shouting, "Jesus saves!" When she stopped at the bookstore to

purchase a Bible, she cringed when the woman at the counter said, "May God bless your reading of His word."

"We didn't take you for one of those Bible thumpers?" her co-workers pointed at her and said when they saw her walk in with the Bible.

Kyle answered, "It's not mine; it's for my Grandma's birthday. She's one of them."

Immediately she was ashamed of herself. She felt like the one black sheep among pure white lambs. She walked around feeling guilty all day. When she got home, she tried to read her Bible, but she did not know where to start, and the shame overwhelmed her.

She heard a still small voice say, "What is it that you truly believe, Kyle?"

"I don't know," she whispered. "I just know that You are real."

She picked up the Bible, and when she opened it, she was at the first chapter of the book of John. She read and mediated for hours, hungry for the impact that the words had on her.

The next day, she walked right by that old man on the corner. This time, when He said, "Jesus saves!" she shouted back, "Amen, brother."

APPLICATION

Kyle felt guilt and shame because she had no integrity. There was no connection between what was going on inside of her and the way she acted. Which one was the fake one? Neither was fake. Kyle, like all of us, was in a battle between her flesh and her spirit. It is an ongoing battle where each of us has to decide if Jesus is enough or if we need something more.

The only way to win this battle is to use the weapons of our warfare to bring down strongholds. These weapons are the word of God, prayer, and the divine aid of the Holy Spirit. Every day we should meditate on the word of God until He gives us something for the day. Every day we should pray without ceasing, and when the Holy Spirit nudges us toward God, we should go with Him and not the way of the world.

If we follow God, we will grow in the gift of faith with integrity of mind, body, and soul. Faith is given to us every time God's word endures and manifests as truth in our lives. Faith grows every time He is faithful when we are faithless. Faith grows every time His grace and mercy follow us. Every time we sense His presence, our faith grows.

P R A Y E R

Father God, I thank You that the integrity of the spirit to falls on me, oh Lord. I thank You that it binds together my mind, body, and soul so that I am one with You. I thank You that this is an adventurous journey on which You will guide my feet. In Jesus' name, Amen.

AUGUST
WEEK 9

DAY 1
A MOUTH THAT SPEAKS LIFE

Did you mean to say that?

"For he that will love life, and see good days, let him refrain his tongue from evil, and his lips that they speak no guile."
(I PETER 3:10)

STORY

Audra sat at the kitchen table in her Grandmother Elaine's kitchen, surrounded not only by the love of her grandmother and three great-aunts, but also by the sweet, mouth-watering aroma of the two lemon pound cakes that were minutes from being pulled from the oven.

Their family reunion was only two days away, and everyone depended on the Walls sisters to fill the dessert table with the baked goods that had been recognized as their specialty for generations.

"I hope that's someone bringing us dinner," Audra said, standing when the doorbell rang. "We've been so busy baking cakes that we didn't think about cooking anything else. I wouldn't mind some crab cakes and a salad."

"You and me both," her grandmother agreed.

Audra opened the door and the smile on her face faded. She blinked, hoping that it was a mirage, but she could tell by the pounding in her chest that the man she hadn't laid eyes on in fifteen years had returned to the same porch stoop where she'd last seen him.

"Hey, baby girl," her dad said. He looked the same, but he had a new set of wrinkles around his eyes and his once black hair was now peppered with gray.

Audra could not stop the single tear that traveled down her cheek.

"I never wanted to see you again!" Audra yelled. She slammed the door, leaving her father outside. She peeked through the side of the curtain until he walked away, got in his car, and disappeared down the street.

APPLICATION

Life has its share of unpredictable and upsetting circumstances. We may find ourselves lugging the emotional baggage of hurt and resentment over a situation we thought we had left behind. When approached about the subject, it is tempting to speak ill of the person who has offended and hurt us. Our words that are meant to harm others, but they really uncover the sin in our heart. The word of God admonishes us to use our words to speak life and not death. It teaches us that our pleasant words can be sweet to our soul and health to our bones like a honeycomb. It also warns us that harsh words stir up anger. The old adage "Sticks and stones may break my bones but words will never hurt me" is far from the truth. Words have the power to hurt, but they also possess the power to heal.

We should be intentional with what we say to others as well as how we frame our own worlds with our words. When you notice negative conversations and thoughts, find things that are positive and uplifting. Make a practice of reciting daily affirmations and memorizing scriptures.

PRAYER

Lord, when I am faced with unexpected circumstances, let me turn to You. Nothing takes You by surprise. When I am caught off guard, I pray that You will calm my thoughts and bring peace to my anxieties. Your word says that all things work together for my good, so I trust You that You have put together the pieces of my life how You see fit. You have orchestrated my life so that I my faith in You increases, and I find strength through You in areas where I would have been weak. Guard my mouth so my words will not bring destruction to hopes and dreams. Let my mouth be used to exalt and edify Your name and encourage others. Help me to see Your children the way You see them, so that I will say what You desire me to say. Amen.

DAY 2

EARS THAT HEAR GOD'S VOICE

Whose voice do you hear?

"Bow down thine ear, and hear the words of the wise, and apply thine heart unto my knowledge."
(PROVERBS 22:17)

STORY

Well who was it?" Grandmother Elaine asked when Audra returned. Despite the earlier complaints of the arthritis that ached her knees, she stood up as soon as she saw Audra's flustered face.

"It was Richard Bellote," Audra said.

"The only man I know by that name is your daddy," her grandmother said, raising her eyebrows. "And I know you're not disrespecting him by using his name in that manner. He's still your father." Looking past Audra, she asked, "Well, where is he?"

"Gone," Audra said, reclaiming her seat in front of a carton of cracked eggs and sifted flour.

"You have every right to feel whatever you're feeling right now," her Aunt Pat consoled. "A man shouldn't walk in and out of your life whenever he sees fit. Even if that man is your dad."

"But you have one Father who's never left you, and that's who you need to depend on right now," Grandma Elaine said. "You know what the word of God says about forgiveness. You cannot just hear it and not do it. The Bible isn't just for reading; it's for living, too."

APPLICATION

We have all been in a situation where we seek refuge and advice from a friend who will undoubtedly agree with our opinion and our misery. Their loyalty to us may rob of us an opportunity to be told the truth in love, stunting a chance to grow into the likeness of God. We should seek friends whose consolation aligns with the thoughts of God. Our conversations with family members should edify Christ and offer biblical insight. Above all, our personal prayer and devotion time with the Lord will bring clarity, peace, and an incomparable wisdom that only He can provide.

The Bible tells us that if we ask for wisdom, God freely and liberally gives it to us. Every area of our lives can be improved with wisdom. Of all of the material possessions that King Solomon could have requested from God, he asked for wisdom. The Bible teaches us through many examples the importance of seeking wisdom. After the death of her husband and father-in-law, Ruth exercised wisdom in following her mother-in-law, Naomi, to Bethlehem, which eventually led her to marrying Boaz. Queen Esther fasted for wisdom as to how to approach King Xerxes, and ultimately saved her people/nation. In all that you do, seek God's wisdom.

Who are you closest confidantes? Where can you go to receive sound counsel, and how dependable are you to offer wisdom?

PRAYER

God, there are many voices and distractions that drown out Your still small voice. Surround me with people who can bring wisdom and correction. I pray that I seek Your way above all others. When things around me change and my circumstances seem insurmountable, You stay steadfast and unchanging in my life. I thank You for being constant. Thank You for a love that never wavers or wanes. Thank You that for loving me despite all of my shortcomings and failures. Amen.

DAY 3

EYES THAT SEE HIS PROMISES

Are you focused on God's plan for your life?

"For I know thoughts that I think toward you, saith the LORD, thoughts of peace, and not of evil, to give you an expected end."
(JEREMIAH 29:11)

STORY

Audra opened the storage chest that was tucked in the back of her closet. In it were her journals, some of her most prized possessions. She had scribbled across the pages, pouring out her heart about everything imaginable since she was in third grade. Over the years, the dreams of a little girl had turned into the prayers of a maturing woman. Each journal was labeled with the year, and she pulled out the pink leather-bound journal from fifteen years ago. She instinctively flipped to almost the exact page where she had written a prayer asking God to restore the relationship with her father. For years, she had wanted him to return. She had prayed. God had answered. Yet and still, she did not expect an answered prayer to take this long, and definitely not to bring this much pain. Audra had to trust in God's timing, even when she did not understand it.

Audra fell to her knees inside of the closet and let the tears flow. "Why now, God? I thought seeing him again would feel better than this, but I feel betrayed," she said in a faint whisper.

She replayed scenes in her head, the one from fifteen years ago and the one from the day before. The little girl inside of her wanted to fall into her daddy's arms to experience all of the love she had missed. She stood and dried her eyes.

Grandma Elaine called to give her the number from a piece of paper she had discovered taped to her door that morning. Audra inhaled deeply before reaching for her cell phone. She had a call to make.

APPLICATION

Rest assured that God has great plans for our lives. He uses every experience, both good and bad, to weave together a beautiful tapestry so others can see His handiwork in our lives. God's plan is to give us a hope and a future and for us to have a life that exceeds more than our expectations.

Our prayers to God are not unheard. In fact, the omnipotent Father knows our unspoken thoughts and the desires of our hearts. When we fully yield our lives to Him, we give Him permission to supersede our limited will with His divine and omniscient insight.

Prayer is a constant open line of communication with our Father. As we establish a consistent prayer life and find peace in His presence, we are able to discern His voice. In His loving way, He convicts us of our transgressions and extends grace for us to repent.

If you are not already doing so, consider keeping a journal of prayers. When you look back, it will serve as a beautiful reminder of God's faith and love for you. Future generations who peruse its pages will be strengthened by reading accounts of a life orchestrated by God.

In times of uncertainty, focus on God's promises, not your problems.

PRAYER

Lord God, thank You for the way You have orchestrated my life. Although I have plans of my own, let it be Your plan that prevails. Light the path for my feet to follow so that I can abide in the shadow of the Almighty. My trust and confidence is in You. Therefore, I will be like a tree deeply rooted by the waters. When turbulent winds blow about me, I will not waver. I will remain steadfast and stand on Your promises. Help me to keep my eyes on You. Even though man has failed me before, You have never forsaken me. Amen.

DAY 4

A HEART THAT FORGIVES OTHERS

Will you let go of your past so you can embrace your future?

"Let all bitterness, and wrath, and anger, and clamour, and evil speaking, be put away from you, with all malice: And be ye kind one to another, tenderhearted, forgiving one another, even as God for Christ's sake hath forgiven you."
(EPHESIANS 4:31–32)

STORY

Audra arrived at the restaurant a few minutes ahead of schedule so that she would have time to settle her nerves. She had followed the

waiter into a quaint corner and ordered a basket of buttermilk biscuits for the table while she waited. It was a love that both she and her dad had shared.

She had been so engrossed with the menu that she did not notice him approach.

"I'm sorry," spilled from his mouth before she had a chance to speak. "I know it will take time, but I hope you can find it in your heart to forgive me," he said.

Audra was thankful that they had met before the lunch rush because her emotions were welling to the surface. She stood, burying her face in her father's chest. She had questions, so many of them, but what she needed now more than anything was that he cared enough to come back to her. Today, she wanted to accept the gift that God had sent her in the return of her father. She had no time to worry about yesterday or even the next day. Her mind was on the present.

"Let's take it one day at a time, Dad," Audra said. "Can we do that?" she asked.

"Of course, we can." He kissed the top of her hair before pulling out her chair.

"I ordered biscuits," Audra said when the waiter approached warily, as if he was interrupting a private moment.

They laughed together, and at that moment, Audra was grateful that some things never changed.

APPLICATION

Jesus gave us an example of ultimate forgiveness. Even with the breath leaving His body, He forgave those who crucified Him. The Bible tells us that when we confess our sins, He is faithful and just to forgive us. As we press toward having the character of Christ, we should forgive others. The act of forgiveness does not mean the person is not guilty, but it opens the path to our healing and it helps to heal others.

Think of a time when you may have knowingly or unknowingly offended another. You may have felt remorse, shame, or even experienced physical discomfort at the realization that you hurt someone else. Now, reflect on how it felt when that same person extended the hand of grace to you. Releasing yourself and others of past offenses leaves your hands free to embrace a future full of hope.

PRAYER

Dear Heavenly Father, thank You for the opportunity to cleanse my heart from bitterness that I harbor against others. I pray that I can extend grace to others the way that You so freely extend it to me. Your everlasting love has sustained and protected me. Let my soul be refreshed. Let my heart be attentive to Your ways. Search my heart and purge it from anything that is not like You. Amen.

HANDS THAT EXTEND GOD'S LOVE

How can you show God's love to another?

*"But to do good and to communicate forget not:
for with such sacrifices God is well pleased."*
(HEBREWS 13:16)

STORY

Audra looked across green fields of grass as plush as carpet. Hundred-year-old oaks towered in the sky, giving shade to the family members who set up their tables and blankets to enjoy the annual family gathering. She spotted her Dad before he saw her, the distinctive sway of his stride making him stand out among a throng of other men. Heads began to turn as people recognized him. They knew how he had disappeared from Audra's life, but their embraces as he walked through the crowd broke every negative thought they may have held against him. When he finally made it to her side, her father had tears streaming down his face.

"I didn't know what to expect when you invited me," he said. "I was willing to take a chance." Running a hand across his face, he said, "Your mom's family took me in from day one. I never should have..."

"Today is a new day," Audra said, interrupting her dad.

She reached under the dessert table for the gift she had brought for him. She had planned on waiting until later, but this seemed to be the perfect time.

"This is for you," Audra said, handing him a framed copy of the journal page of her prayer.

"The only thing better than this is a slice of your grandma's lemon pound cake," he laughed as he pulled his daughter into his arms.

Audra beckoned for Grandma Elaine. "Coming right up," her grandmother shouted.

APPLICATION

As Christians, we are to be the hands and feet of Jesus on earth. The greatest commandment is to love the Lord our God with all of your heart, mind, and strength. It is a blessing to seek ways to show God's love to others. You can show your love to others in many ways. One week, it may look like a card mailed to a relative in a nursing home and another week love may be found in extra moments of bedside hugs with a toddler who has been cranky all day. You can show God's love by delivering meals to a family in a financial bind or providing care packets to a homeless shelter. Love is action.

Take the time to think about those around you who may need to experience God's love through you. What acts of kindness can you do to bless others?

PRAYER

Father God, there is no greater love than Your love for me. It extends beyond what my mind can comprehend, and nothing I say or do can escape it. Every day I will strive to trust You, even in times when I do not understand Your ways. Your word reminds me that my thoughts are not Your thoughts and Your ways are not my ways. Align my will with Yours. Amen.

AUGUST
WEEK 10

DAY 1
A SEASON OF SUFFERING

Will your faith pass this test?

"Who are kept by the power of God through faith u[n] salvation ready to be revealed in the last time. Where[in] ye greatly rejoice, though now for a season, if need be, [ye] are in heaviness through manifold temptations: That [the] trial of your faith, being more precious than of gold th[at] perisheth, though it be tried with fire, might be foun[d] unto praise and honour and glory at the appearing [of] Jesus Christ."

(I PETER 1:5-7)

STORY

Shanté was in total disbelief as the nurse delivered the news of her daughter's death. She had spent the past two years going back an[d] forth to doctors' offices with Aaliyah. Over

that time, they had become very close. The routine was singing along to praise and worship music in the car on the way to appointments and lifting prayers of faith on the way back home.

As she listened to Nurse Jackie, the words began to resemble the famous "wah wah" voice of the Peanuts gang's beloved teacher Miss Othmar.

"Nooooo! I just want to see my baby!" Shanté cried out.

APPLICATION

No parent wants to bury a child. However, it is a devastating reality for many. For those of us who have had a season of suffering come our way, the pain at times seems unbearable. Because grief is unique to the individual experiencing it, no two people handle it the same. When we experience loss, so many existential questions cross our minds regarding the meaning of life and faith. If what we prayed so diligently for does not manifest, it can cause us to doubt God's plan.

So, what do we do when our faith is tested? Faith without doubt is certainty. Experience teaches us early on that uncertainty is a part of life. The good news is that faith and doubt can exist at the same time. When doubt creeps in, do not despair. Hold on to your faith. The Bible teaches that perseverance through trials will cause our faith to mature and deepen over time.

PRAYER

God of all comfort, when grief and loss get the best of me, I need Your awesome power to guard my faith. When I was a child, the seasoned saints would say, "God will keep you if you want to be kept." Lord, this has become my testimony. Help me to keep the faith as I offer You the pain I feel in exchange for Your comfort. Thank You for the prayers of the ancestors. They hold me up when my strength is fading. In the incomparable name of Jesus, Amen!

DAY 2
THE STORM IS RAGING

Who is my help in times of trouble?

"I will lift up mine eyes unto the hills, from whence cometh my help. My help cometh from the LORD, which made heaven and earth. He will not suffer thy foot to be moved: he that keepeth thee will not slumber. Behold, he that keepeth Israel shall neither slumber nor sleep."

(PSALM 121:1-4)

STORY

Her screams could be heard clear across the entire fourth floor.

"I'm sorry. I'm so very sorry," whispered Nurse Jackie.

Shanté was inconsolable. A storm of doubt and

183

shame began to rage around her. Thoughts raced through her mind like a runaway train.

"Maybe, I should have brought her to the hospital earlier," she thought. "If only I had prayed harder, my child would still be alive. Lola's child recovered from her illness, why didn't mine?"

Suddenly, she remembered the lyrics of the song she led at church on Sunday, and a peace fell over her. Moments later, Shanté walked toward the hospital bed and noticed that Aaliyah looked so beautiful. She smiled and reminisced about the day her daughter was born. Nurse Jackie made a pronouncement of death and turned to wrap her arms around Shanté. The grief fog began to set in, and time seemed to stand still as the tears streamed down her cheeks.

APPLICATION

The death of a child at any age is a painfully difficult experience. Studies suggest that parents of children who die, regardless of the cause, are likely to suffer from symptoms of traumatic stress as well as the classic of psychological, biological, and social responses to grief. Research related to the biological impact of trauma indicates that the devastating effects of it change brain structure, neural pathways, hormones, toxin elimination, the nervous system, the immune system, brain neurotransmitters, and cells.

When the worst thing that can happen happens to you, it alters your DNA. I am so glad that Jesus knows what it is like to grieve. Jesus groaned in the spirit, felt troubled, and wept. If you are experiencing grief and loss, cry out to him. He is bigger than your storm. He can bear your pain.

PRAYER

Jehovah Rophe, my tears have become my food. You know the effects of my mental health trauma better than I do. Please heal and restore me. You did it for the children of Israel when they needed to be healed. Do it for me, God. In Jesus name, Amen!

DAY 3

THIS TOO SHALL PASS

When will my heart stop breaking?

"It is better to go to the house of mourning, than to go to the house of feasting: for that is the end of all men; and the living will lay it to his heart. Sorrow is better than laughter: for by the sadness of the countenance the heart is made better."

(ECCLESIASTES 7:2-3)

STORY

The house was eerily cold and quiet when Shanté made it home that evening. She began calling family members and friends to let them know that Aaliyah had transitioned. She also called her pastor. He prayed a prayer of comfort for her and the family, assuring her that

her church family would be there every step of the way. Soon, friends and family began to show up at her doorstep. She needed their presence; it all seemed so surreal.

Stories were shared. Memories were recollected. As the evening progressed, Shanté disappeared to her bedroom. She fell on the bed in the grips of a pain that felt like an elephant was balancing on one leg on top of her chest. She had been grieving for almost two years, since Aaliyah had been first diagnosed. This heartbreak was unconscionable. She cried, "Lord, have mercy!" as she grabbed her chest.

APPLICATION

How is sorrow better than laughter? Often times our greatest sorrows cause us to look more seriously at our need for God. When we do not have anywhere else to turn, we begin to rely on His strength in our weakness.

Sorrow can also cause us to reflect on the difficulties in our lives and to evaluate our situations. Maybe you have been contemplating making a change in a relationship that is toxic or a job where you are the target of gas lighting. To avoid the change, you find yourself engaged in activities that are lighthearted and fun. Laughter may provide a temporary escape, but if you do not deal with your grief, your grief will deal with you. When you are tested in ways that are too grueling to even think about, let go of the outcome you envision and let God manifest His will.

PRAYER

King of my heart, my house is a house of mourning, but You still rule and reign. Thank You for the body of Christ at large and, specifically, the women of color who seek Your face along with me. You comfort me in all my tribulation that I may be able to comfort those who are in trouble as God comforts me. In the matchless name of Jesus, I pray. Amen!

DAY 4

NOTHING IS FOR NOTHING

What is the purpose of this pain?

"Now they which were scattered abroad upon the persecution that arose about Stephen travelled as far as Phenice, and Cyprus, and Antioch, preaching the word to none but unto the Jews only. And some of them were men of Cyprus and Cyrene, which, when they were come to Antioch, spake unto the Grecians, preaching the LORD Jesus. And the hand of the LORD was with them: and a great number believed, and turned unto the LORD."
(ACTS 11:19–21)

STORY

Shanté and her parents sat at the dining room table, sorting through pictures of Aaliyah for the obituary. Her modern ranch style house with minimalist décor was jam-packed; there were people in every nook and cranny. Neighbors and friends provided a steady supply of food, beverages, and paper goods. When her best friend arrived with a veggie plate from her favorite Ethiopian restaurant, she realized she had not eaten all day. Frankly, she just did not have much of an appetite these days.

To her surprise, Aaliyah's friends decided to take four-hour shifts at the house to sit with Momma Shanté, as they affectionately called her. Their thoughtfulness and empathy were a sweet blessing. Each one shared about how Aaliyah lived her faith in Christ out loud. They read text messages and social media posts that she sent to them encouraging them to press toward the mark, despite her own suffering from a debilitating illness. Aaliyah found a purpose in her pain.

APPLICATION

The early church was persecuted for preaching about Christ. When Stephen was killed, the church scattered. His death became a turning point in Christianity. Jewish believers began speaking to Greek-speaking Gentiles as well as Jews, and many believed.

We have all been to funerals where people accept Christ. In a manner of speaking, our loved one's death leads to spiritual life. The Bible teaches that unless a grain of wheat falls into the earth and dies, it remains alone. If it dies, it bears much fruit. The Christian church grew out of trauma and hardship. If we persevere, we will grow too!

PRAYER

Giver of every perfect gift from above, thank You for revelation and wisdom. Daily, You show me the purpose of my pain. I know that everything happens for a reason. It is a great exchange! I give You my pain and You give me Your peace. Help me to persevere through the trials and tribulations that life brings. Thank You for loving, keeping and comforting me. You are my portion and my inheritance. Amen.

DAY 5

FINALLY, IT IS OVER

Why did God bring you out?

"For thou, O God, hast proved us: thou hast tried us, as silver is tried. Thou broughtest us into the net; thou laidst affliction upon our loins. Thou hast caused men to ride over our heads; we went through fire and through water: but though broughtest us out into a wealthy place."

(PSALM 66:10-12)

STORY

The atmosphere in the sanctuary of Mt. Zion was celestial. As the associate minister read the Summary of Life, tears began to well in Shanté's eyes. How on earth was she able to capture sixteen years of life experiences in four

paragraphs? Aaliyah's friend Shay sang, and the Holy Spirit moved with power through each aisle. Aaliyah did not remember much after that.

When they arrived at the graveside, the sun was setting over the horizon. The family was seated and given white roses to place on the casket for the interment. The Pastor stated that Aaliyah would not have to suffer anymore because there is no pain or sorrow in heaven. Shanté would recall that statement many, many times as the days, weeks, and months passed.

Shanté went to grief counseling to learn to cope with her physical, cognitive, social, spiritual, and emotional responses to the loss of her child. She was still learning to live with the loss and to accept that Aaliyah's physical pain was over, but that the love she had for her would never end.

APPLICATION

My sister, the pain we experience in grief and loss is the cost of caring, but what is life without it? At the core of our deepest emotions are the beliefs that drive them. We must ask ourselves if we really believe that God will deliver us from our affliction.

When we cannot understand God's ways, we have to choose to trust in Him, knowing that we shall see the glory of God eventually. Press on and do not give up!

PRAYER

Heavenly Father, I believe You when You say that I am blessed, chosen, holy, blameless, loved, adopted, free, forgiven, and accepted. You brought me out of the fire and water, and I am still standing. I will declare Your goodness in the land of the living. I know that You will cause even my hurts to work out for good. To the glory of God, Amen!

AUGUST
WEEK 11

DAY 1

THRIVING IN YOUR BEAUTY

Do you know your worth in Christ?

"For we are his workmanship, created in Christ Jesus to do good works, which God prepared beforehand, that we should walk in them."
(EPHESIANS 2:10, ESV)

STORY

Nicole was excited because she was headed to her first Women's Bible Study group. This would provide a great opportunity for the women of the church to learn more about God and fellowship with each other. As Nicole entered, she greeted everyone with a smile and a hug. The first lady, Cathy, the leader of the study group, welcomed her.

The women eagerly gathered around the table when Cathy excitedly asked, "Do you know your worth?"

There was a moment of silence in the room. She asked the question again. She received a few responses, but many were still quiet. She then passed around a beautiful quilt that her grandmother made. Next, she passed around a jewelry box full of valuable jewels. Last, she passed each woman a shiny mirror. She explained to them why the three items were important and valuable.

"This beautiful handmade quilt is unique because my grandmother made it specifically for me," she boasted. "This jewelry box is valuable because it contains precious diamonds, other gems, and has monetary value. I gave each of you a shiny mirror. I want to know what you think it represents. What do you see? Do you see your flaws or imperfections?"

"I want you all to see your beauty and worth in Christ," Cathy concluded. "God sees us all as His masterpiece because we are all fearfully and wonderfully made. God considers us His precious and cherished treasures. Even with our differences, we are all worthy and beautiful in His sight.

APPLICATION

Sometimes, women may have difficulty knowing their value or worth in life because of self-esteem or confidence issues, past experiences, or others' thoughts of them. However, knowing your worth begins with understanding who you are to Christ. You are worthy in every aspect to God. You do not have to doubt God. You are and will always be enough to Him. You are more precious than rubies. You were specially created by God, loved by God, and valued by God. When you look in the mirror, you can say with confidence, "I am worthy; I am enough and God made me this way on purpose."

PRAYER

Lord, I am grateful that I am worthy in Your eyes and that You love me more than anyone else loves me. My heart smiles to know that I can do all things when I put my trust in You. As a believer, I am confident that I am who You say that I am. Thank You for loving me and calling me Your own. Amen.

DAY 2
THRIVING IN GOD'S WILL

Are you living a life that is pleasing to God?

"But be consistent to seek God first every day, and He will make your ways successful!"

(JOSHUA 1:7-9)

STORY

Let me see what's on my list today," says Nicole.

Nicole is a proud mother of three and a dedicated wife. She takes pride in being organized and making good use of every minute of her day. She lives by her daily planners, wall calendars, and cute little Post-it notes! She gets up in

the morning preparing her to-do-lists and scheduling the kids' practices, meetings, outings, dinner, and other activities. She feels delighted when she fills up her planner.

One day, while picking up her daughter Zion from choir rehearsal, she asked, "Mom when do you schedule time with God?"

Nicole quickly answered, "Every day!"

This question from her ten-year-old caught Nicole off guard. Truthfully, her daughter's question really hit home for her. That night she wrote "Quality Time with God!" in her planner. She wanted to make a conscious decision to become committed to putting God first over everything Not only did she want to be a good example for her family, but she also wanted to live a life that was pleasing to God.

APPLICATION

Just like Nicole, we need to reflect on getting our priorities in order and determine what we consider important in life. As Christians, we all should want to grow and mature in Christ. Our goal should be to please God, not man. Just as plants need soil, water, and sunlight to grow, we need a biblical foundation, godly instructions, and fellowship with fellow believers to thrive in Christ. In order to grow, we must desire to seek God every day. We can thrive by getting to know Him, trusting Him, and thriving to please Him. God wants us to give our lives to Him. In God, we will always thrive.

PRAYER

Lord, I pray that You continue to help me thrive and not just survive in my Christian journey. I pray that my knowledge, faith, and confidence grow stronger in You. I know You are the true vine, and I am the branches that get pruned. I am yearning to grow, learn, and yield to doing what is right. I want to live a life that is pleasing to You, Lord. I pray that I grow day by day to be more like You. Amen.

DAY 3
THRIVING IN YOUR PURPOSE

Does your vision for life align with God's plans?

"Many are the plans in a person's heart, but it is the LORD's purpose that prevails."
(PROVERBS 19:21, NIV)

STORY

Nicole listened to her daughter Zion explain her vision board during her monthly youth group meeting. She was amazed at the words and phrases that she used to so passionately describe her project. However, the words that stood out the most were "growth" and "walk by faith." Nicole felt a small sense of joy that she might be doing a little something right as Zion's mother because her daughter knew that God was in control. After the meeting was over, Nicole eagerly encouraged Zion to keep her hope and faith in God because He controls her future.

APPLICATION

The vision board and dream board craze has been popular for over a decade. It provides an opportunity for individuals to put their hopes and dreams in a format that that can be seen with the intent to make each goal a reality. You may use these boards as a positive road map to achieve future goals, although they may not all come to fruition.

Well, we should not fret when things do not happen as we would like because delayed does not mean denied. We serve a God who looks out for our best interests. God informs us that we may have plans of our own, but His purpose prevails. We must put our faith in God and allow Him to lead us in our future endeavors and direct our paths. God knows and wants what is best for His children!

PRAYER

Lord God, I thank You for being all knowing and all-powerful. No matter what plans I have for my future, You are in control. I am grateful that You provide opportunities and blessings for me daily, even ones I do not deserve. I know that You listen and care about all of my wants and needs. I want to continue to lean and depend on You, Lord, to direct my path. I am confident that I can thrive in my purpose when I put my faith in You. Amen.

DAY 4

THRIVING THROUGH UNEXPECTED TIMES

How can you persevere through unexpected circumstances?

"Cast all your anxiety on him because he cares for you."
(*I PETER 5:7, NIV*)

STORY

Nicole and her husband Phil sat nervously awaiting the MRI results. Phil had already been out for six weeks due to a motor vehicle accident that resulted in a cervical fracture in his neck. This unexpected event turned their lives upside down.

Dr. Allen came out and stated, "I'm sorry. The fusion was not successful, and you will need another procedure. Six additional weeks of recovery will be necessary.

This news was devastating to Nicole and Phil.

With tears rolling down her face, Nicole looked at her husband asking, "What are we going to do now?"

There were so many challenges Nicole was already facing, such as her husband's newly acquired disability, his loss of independence, and the loss of family income. She was also raising a newborn baby in the midst of all of this. Phil was not physically able to assist her with the baby as he had before his injury.

Nicole called her mom to discuss the results. After hearing the results, her mom, Willa, immediately reassured her that they would get through this with the help of the Lord. She reminded Nicole that we are never alone. God will never leave us or forsake us.

Nicole and Phil decided to stand firm on God's word and put their faith in Him to see them through every trial and tribulation.

Twelve weeks later, Nicole and Phil were back at the doctor's office awaiting the results.

Dr. Allen walked in and stated, "Phil, I can now release you from my care and you can return to work on light duty."

They were both overwhelmed with joy. Nicole began praising the Lord, right then and there. She was not ashamed to worship and give praise and honor to God.

APPLICATION

In life, you will face challenging and unexpected situations that cause you to feel alone and unsure of what to do. Challenges are a part of everyday life, but they make us stronger. God gives strength to the weary. No matter the circumstances, God is in control. We need to understand that the battle is not ours. It is the Lord's! We are not alone.

Nothing catches God by surprise. That is why we have to give our lives, our situations, and our circumstances to Him. We have to trust in God's promises and provisions for our lives. Continue to put your trust and hope in God. Through it all, you can still thrive during the unexpected times and have joy in the midst of it all. God is faithful and will give us the victory.

PRAYER

Lord God, even in times of uncertainty, I can find comfort in believing in You. When I am discouraged or feel that there is no way out, I will still trust You. I pray that You continue to be the head of my life and give me the knowledge to be obedient, faithful, and confident in You. I know that You are my way maker, promise keeper, and work on my behalf even when I do not see it. When I feel overwhelmed or anxious, I can lean and depend on You. I am grateful to You, Lord, for never leaving me during times of uncertainty or difficulty. Amen.

DAY 5

LEADING OTHERS TO THRIVE

Do you help others to thrive?

"Do not neglect to do good and to share what you have, for such sacrifices are pleasing to God."

STORY

Nicole enjoyed seeing the excitement in the graduates' faces as they walked across the stage to receive their diploma. She was relieved that graduation day and another school year were a success. Nicole had recently begun to question her career as a teacher, wondering if she was still making a difference in her students'

lives. As the program ended, she heard someone calling her name. It was her student, Laura.

Laura shouted, "Wait, Mrs. Nicole! I want to give you something."

To Nicole's surprise, Laura handed her professor a gift and a card. When Nicole got in the car, she decided to open the gift and card. She smiled as she read the card.

"Dear Mrs. Nicole, I want to thank you for believing in me from day one. I did not think I would make it this far, but you believed in me! I appreciate how you encouraged and guided me over the years, so I could be successful. Please keep teaching because you make a difference!"

After reading the card, Nicole was humbled and found confirmation that she was walking in her purpose.

APPLICATION

Do you remember who influenced you in life? Was it a parent, teacher, mentor, or the author of an inspirational book? Those individuals can be considered game changers. Are you one? Just as Nicole helped change her student's life, you can help lead others to Christ. As a believer in Christ, you should strive to help others to reach their potential. You should desire Christ to live through you. Have you ever thought that letting your light shine could lead unbelievers to Christ? You should strive to bless others so they can thrive in life as well.

PRAYER

Lord, I thank You for my gifts and talents which are blessings from You. I appreciate the calling You have given me, and I pray for Your guidance on how to use my gifts daily. Allow me to show love, give hope, and bless others like You bless me abundantly each day. Allow me to use gentle and encouraging words to lift others up and sow good seeds. I pray that I can remain humble and obedient in keeping Your word. I pray that I can continue to help others thrive. Keep using me in whatever manner You see fit, Lord. Amen.

AUGUST
WEEK 12

DAY 1
IT'S YOUR PEACE

Why are you fighting?

*"Then he answered and spake unto me, saying,
This is the word of the LORD unto Zerubbabel,
saying, Not by might, nor by power,
but by my spirit, saith the LORD of hosts."*

(ZECHARIAH 4:6)

STORY

Harper grew up feeling as though she had to fight for everything.

"Nothing is going to be easy for you," she was told as a child. "You are going to have to work twice as hard as everyone else just to get half as much."

With these words etched in her mind and her spirit, life became a series of obstacles to be overcome, not something to be experienced in an abundant and joyful manner. In her mind, life was one big fight. To make sure she succeeded, Harper became an overachiever. Her close friends would joke that she "overdid" everything. She spent days on assignments that everyone else finished in only a couple of hours.

This seemed to be a good trait, though, because it worked. Harper graduated at the top of her high school class. She was also a star athlete and class president. She won a scholarship to attend an impressive university, where she was on the Dean's List every semester, a member of the volleyball team, and a campus leader. Great accomplishments would became her survival mechanism. Overdoing was her way of ensuring that she overcame the obstacles in life. She approached every goal, every task, and every assignment as though she was in the fight of her life.

APPLICATION

Does this story sound familiar? How many Harpers do you know? Maybe there is a Harper within you. Are you highly driven, hyper-focused, and successful by the world's standards? Do you approach everything as a battle to be won? People probably say that you are a perfectionist, a title that you wear like a badge of honor. You may have been called controlling, which can be detrimental.

It is fine to be driven. It is the fighting and laboring done in the absence of God's direction, grace, and protection that can get you into trouble. Fighting creates stress, anxiety, sleepless nights, and emptiness. When you are driven to reach externally gratifying goals and not the will of God, you often end up tired, frustrated and possibly in places where you have no desire to be.

Fighting for jobs, relationships, and a myriad of external matters is a waste of time because the real fight is an internal fight for your peace, your sanity, and God's grace over your life. The beauty is that this actually is not a fight at all. It is something that must be prioritized. If it is, prioritized, then you will see just how masterfully God works out every detail of your life. Replace your controlling spirit with the shield of faith. You do not have to fight for your life. God will do that for you, if you let Him.

PRAYER

Help me Father to depend on You with every fiber of my being, for every aspect of my life. Help me always remember that there is no fight in this world that I have to undertake on my own. Though I respect the virtues of hard work and determination, let me not rely on them alone for our success in life, lest I open the door for the enemy to detract and distract me from living for You. Let me not create definitions of success in ways that do not include You, and help me to realize that my successes will come not only from the work of my hands, but by the mighty power of Your spirit guiding and protecting me along the way. Amen.

IT'S YOUR NECESSITY

Do you see what He sees?

*"Wherefore take unto you the whole armour of God,
that ye may be able to withstand in the evil day,
and having done all, to stand."*
(*EPHESIANS 6:13*)

STORY

Even though Harper was a born-again believer, there were things that she did not know about what it meant to truly walk in faith. She tried her best to live right and not sin against God. She read the Bible and attended church, but she did not know how to invoke the power of the Lord into every nuance of her life, especially

her educational and professional goals. That, she thought, she had to figure out on her own.

When life got hard, Harper's first response was to dig in—work more, study more, and solicit more advice. She did not turn to God for help. She did not pay more. This approach was not only draining, but it began to wreak havoc on her mental health. She constantly overextended herself to prove something and to please others. She still sometimes did not get the results she desired. Before she knew it, Harper doubted herself and battled depressing thoughts, all because she tried to do everything on her own.

APPLICATION

You cannot do everything on your own without ending up mentally exhausted. You do not have to it alone. Trust and rest in knowing that the omniscience of God is your survival guide; it is the ultimate life hack! Always remember the saying "I don't know what the future holds, but I know who holds the future." God knows all, so you have to learn to trust in Him completely! Once you embrace this, you will know how turn to God as your first line of defense in every situation. Seek His face and seek His guidance. Let the Holy Spirit move you from victory to victory.

The armor of God equips you for every battle in life; even the everyday battles of school and work that are so practical you think you can or should deal with them alone. There is nothing that you should face alone! Life will throw you some rough waves, but, with God, you will emerge from them standing tall and riding gracefully into calm waters. Where your own knowledge and strength may fail, the armor of God is infallible. You will always win with God on your side. Remain close to Him for strategy, insight, divine connection, right responses, course corrections, and everything that is required for successful day-to-day living.

PRAYER

Dear God, help me to understand Your desire and willingness to abide with me on a daily basis, hour by hour and minute by minute. There is no aspect of my life that is mundane to You. Increase my faith so that I run to You as the first line of defense. You are the ultimate life coach and the winning playmaker. We are nothing without You, and everything with You. I know that the plans that You have for me are plans to prosper me and never to harm me, and I want those plans to come to fruition. I ask You to humble my heart so that I can yield my desires and the limitations of even my own intellect to You, knowing that You will guide me through this life as the ultimate captain of my destiny. Amen.

DAY 3

IT'S YOUR CONFIDENCE

Where can you turn?

*"It is God that girdeth me with strength,
and maketh my way perfect."*

(PSALM 18:32)

STORY

Just give it time, and God will work everything out." These were the words of wisdom that Harper remembered her grandmother saying since she was a little girl. However, Harper rarely operated by God's timing. She was the queen of the SWOT analysis. She was the queen of listing pros and cons. She was the queen of soliciting opinions from people she trusted for advice.

A guidance counselor actually told Harper when she was in college that she had "paralysis of analysis." This happened when she was trying to figure out if she should go to graduate school or accept a job offer that she had received. She labored over the decision until she was sick with anxiety. Harper had to learn the hard way that overthinking will rarely lead to the right answer. She also learned that even well-meaning people whom she trusted could steer her the wrong way. Not everyone knew what was best for her. Really, God was the only one who actually did.

APPLICATION

As you move through life, it is certainly important to seek wise counsel. This is actually a biblical concept. It is prudent to seek advice, gather information and weigh options when it comes to decision making, but prayer needs to be one of the integral steps. So, yes, follow a decision-making process, but never forget that when you really need an answer, God is the one you need to ask for advice. He alone knows what is best for you. If you lack wisdom, seek God, and He will give it generously without reproach.

You have to condition yourself to integrate prayer into your process. Pray and seek God while you are preparing. Gather information. Then pray. Seek wise counsel. Then pray. Do not leave God out! The beauty of learning this lesson is that, through prayer, God will lead you to the right people, guide you to ask the right questions, and release the right resources to make what may have been a difficult decision simple. When you put God in the mix, anxiety and deliberation yield to calm assuredness.

PRAYER

Dear God, forgive me for the times that I have leaned on my own understanding and the advice of others more than I leaned on You. Help me to remember that it is Your guidance that I need the most. You are my way maker, and You have the answers that I am looking for, if only I would ask. Your word says to acknowledge You, and You will direct my path. My intellect is a blessing, and so is my faith. Let me discover how to use both of these gifts so that I can discern the direction that You would have me move in order to stay in Your will. Let my heartfelt prayer always be that Thy will be done, and not my own. Amen.

DAY 4
IT'S YOUR RIGHT

Why are you so heavy?

*"For though we walk in the flesh,
we do not war after the flesh."*
(II CORINTHIANS 10:3)

STORY

Harper had planned to attend graduate school right after college, but the job offer that she received seemed too good to be true. "Graduate school will always be there," she reasoned, as she considered the advice she received from most of those she asked, which was overwhelmingly "take the job." Even though going into the workforce at that time was not the desire of her heart, she made what she thought

was the smartest decision and accepted the job. Harper did not realize that she was not prepared for all that came with this great opportunity, such as moving to a new city, long work hours, and the competitive corporate life.

Harper's decision was smart on paper, but it was not smart for her, and she was miserable. She gave herself three years to stay in this job. She reasoned that she would be able to save money while gaining the experience and cultivating the relationships that would benefit her career goals. Again, it was good on paper, but not good for her.

Before the three years were up, Harper's mental health began to suffer. She moved swiftly from being miserable being depressed. Harper began to feel burdened by life, and it showed.

APPLICATION

There is a way that seems right to man, but that leads to death. Perhaps, like Harper, there is something in your life that seemed right to you. However, now that you are in it, you realize that it is all wrong. Prayerfully, death is not imminent in your case, but disappointment, depression, and despair are your frequent companions. Do not let where you are become your final stop! Reframe your thinking and refocus your attention to align with God's purpose for your life instead of fighting to lead a life that others have designed for you.

God wants you to flourish. God wants you to prosper. God wants you to have life more abundantly, and God wants you to have peace. Let Him be the architect and you will live the life of your dreams, one where you sleep well at night, smile often, and enjoy the fruits of your labor because you are walking in your purpose. Life is not meant to be a burden. Why be so heavily burdened when you can be light as a bird knowing that God has everything under control?

PRAYER

Father, thank You for Your Holy Spirit and for the divine guidance that pricks my heart when I am moving in a direction that is not aligned with Your purpose. Teach me to honor my internal compass that shows me the way. Help me to make decisions that make You proud, even when this may be hard or when it means doing what may be unpopular. Let me establish my standards based on what will bring me the peace of knowing that I am in Your will. Let me remember that life is never a burden when I place You at the head. Give me the courage and the confidence to be led by the Holy Spirit and not by the flesh, even when it does not make sense to other people. Amen.

DAY 5
IT'S YOUR PROTECTION

Who is coming to save you?

*"After these things the word of the LORD
came unto Abram in a vision, saying,
Fear not, Abram: I am thy shield,
and thy exceeding great reward."*

(GENESIS 15:1)

STORY

Depression began to get the best of Harper, and she did not know how to shake herself out of it. How could it be that a great job would cause her so much distress? She was barely meeting her work deadlines, and her boss was treating her horribly. To make matters worse, she was not adjusting well to her new city.

Harper's depression compounded daily, weighing her down like a pile of concrete. She realized that she had made the wrong decision, but how could she, a vibrant star student who was on her way to success, turn this around? If she quit this job, she would have to move back home for a while. She would look like a failure, which was her biggest fear in life. In a moment of despair, Harper cried out to God, and she heard the Holy Spirit whisper, "Your fear is misguided."

It was in that moment that Harper understood her colossal mistake. She put too much emphasis on what other people thought about her. That is what got her in this position in the first place. This clarity provided Harper necessary emotional relief as she began praying about her exit strategy and the steps that she needed to get her life on track God's way.

APPLICATION

Do not be wise in your own eyes. Oh, how much easier said than done! Friend, you need to learn how to do this every single day. Do not be wise in your own eyes! Make this the mantra that you follow so that you do not plan yourself into high places that have low rewards overall. Remember that your reward is a life orchestrated by God's will. The peace of God is your reward. Keeping up appearances, advancing too quickly, or moving in the wrong direction altogether comes at an emotional cost that is simply not worth bearing.

Sorrow, stress, anxiety, and depression are not God's will for your life! Walk valiantly in this knowledge. Always pray to understand the difference between "a" blessing and "your" blessing so that your decision making is purpose driven. Always remember that there is no place that you may find yourself where God is unable to save you. If you do find that you have made a decision that is not good for you, God will help you work your way out of it and into His perfect will. His armor is your protector, and He is your rescuer.

PRAYER

Thank You, Lord, for always coming to save me. Too often, I get myself into situations that only You can help me conquer. Give me a heart that is not too proud to say that I need You. Give me a heart that turns to You first. Break down any spirit of fear or pride that stands in the way of pursuing my best in You. It was You, not other people, who created me in my mother's womb. I bind the spirit of pleasing people and release the spirit of relentless obedience to Your direction and Your word. Where my view is limited, You have no blind spots. There is not a single aspect of my life in which You have no interest. Your word says that even every hair on my head has been counted, so there is no question of Your limitless care for me. Thank You for Your everlasting love and grace. Amen.

AUGUST
WEEK 13

DAY 1
GIVER

Are you a giver or a taker?

*"Every good and perfect gift is from above,
coming down from the Father of the heavenly lights,
who does not change like shifting shadows."*
(JAMES 1:17, NIV)

STORY

Tori was devastated as she ended the phone call from one of her best friends, Asia, who had just told Tori how difficult it was being her friend. She told Tori that she called when she needed something or when she needed help with a problem. She also called when she needed relationship advice. She said that Tori seldom offered to give of herself.

236

Still stunned from the conversation, Tori called another friend, Jamie.

When Jamie answered the phone she said, "Hey Tori, what you need?"

"Why did you answer the phone asking what I needed?" Tori asked.

Jamie replied, "Because you usually need something when you call. That's just the way you are, but I love you though."

At those words, Tori realized that what Asia said was true. She was a taker. The tears began to flow.

APPLICATION

Truth spoken by a friend that helps us understand a truth about ourselves. So many times, we are told to focus on ourselves and get what we want. Me time is a priority, and if we are not sensitive to the Holy Spirit, we will miss the fact that we have become self-centered.

The Holy Spirit is a giver. It is through the gift of the Holy Spirit that we become Christ-like. The Holy Spirit is a gift! If we look at our lives as an opportunity to be a gift to those with whom we come in contact, and if we look at our lives as an opportunity to be a gift to our families and friends, we can model the Holy Spirit's behavior and truly become givers and not takers.

PRAYER

Father God, I submit my will to Yours. Father I admit I have been a taker in my relationships. Father, I ask for forgiveness and that Your Holy Spirit helps me to model Your nature and truly become a giver. Father, help me to see ways I can give to those around me. I thank You for this change in my life. In Jesus Name, Amen!

DAY 2
PEACE

Are you searching for peace?

"Thou will keep him in perfect peace,
whose mind is stayed on thee:
because he trusteth in thee."
(ISAIAH 26:3)

STORY

Asia called Tori and asked if they could talk. Tori was excited that she was meeting Asia for coffee. She was excited because she had been trying to become a giver and she was making a conscious effort to give of herself to her friends and not just take from them.

Asia sat across from Tori and began to share how she had not been able to rest. She had no peace in her life. Her job was becoming more difficult, and she had a new boss who did not seem to value her skills. She was worried. She thought about it all the time, trying to figure out how to fix her work situation. She tried to be more pleasant. She tried to come into work earlier. She tried to work late. She went to sleep at night thinking about a solution to this problem, and she woke every morning thinking about the situation at her job.

Tori listened, took Asia's hand, and said, "You have been searching everywhere for an answer and for peace, except in the word of God, except through the leading of the Holy Spirit. God will keep you in perfect peace if your mind is focused on Him."

Asia led her friend in a prayer for peace.

APPLICATION

Sometimes, we have a problem that seems natural. We consider it a problem that only we can fix. When things are bad in the work place, we try to figure out what we can do in the flesh, how we can change people and how we can we win them over to our side. Before we know it, we have lost our peace! The way back to our peace is to recharge ourselves with God's word and keep our mind on Him. God keeps us in perfect peace. We may still be in difficult situations, but we can have peace in the midst of the situation.

There was a worldwide art competition held in France. Artists from all over the world participated and attended. The challenge was to create a painting that depicted peace. The three finalists entered the room to describe their paintings. The first finalist's painting was of a beautiful sunset with an amazing sky. The sun looked like a calm fireball sinking into the sky. The second finalist's painting was of a beautiful beachfront at a calm ocean with no waves. The still blue water was inviting. The third finalist's painting was of a raging storm. It portrayed the lightning in the sky, the trees bending from the force of the wind and the rain pounding. There, in the midst of the storm, tucked in the side of a rock on the side of the mountain, a bird was feeding her young.

The third finalist won. The other artists were furious; they demanded an explanation. In their opinions, the winning painting was clearly not a depiction of peace. The committee explained to the artists that anyone can be at peace while watching a peaceful sunset. Anyone can have peace sitting at the beach without a cloud in the sky, watching the beautiful calm water. Real peace, in the judges' opinions, is when in the middle of a raging storm, a mother finds a peaceful place to feed her child. Being able to still function and have peace while in a storm is the meaning of real peace.

PRAYER

Father God, Your word says that You will keep me in perfect peace when my mind is on You! Father, I give my work situation to You. Father, I give my mind to thoughts of You and Your word. Keep me, Father, in Your peace. In the mighty and matchless name of Jesus, I pray, Amen.

DAY 3
TRUTH

Are you walking in truth?

*"And ye shall know the truth,
and the truth shall make you free."*
(JOHN 8:32)

STORY

"Jamie, what are you going to do?" asked Tori.

"I don't know. I don't know what's true or not," she shared.

Jamie was in love. Her boyfriend, Amari, was the answer to her prayers. He was kind, handsome, and had an amazing job. Only one thing was missing. He did not attend church, ever! He had been raised in the church, but he had not attended since he returned from college a few

years ago. She believed he knew God. He said he was a believer, but she did not know if that was that true.

Amari was ready for marriage, but Jamie needed to know truth about his relationship with God. She felt as if she were in an impossible situation.

"I feel like a prisoner," Jamie said.

"Jamie, you can know the truth, and the truth will set you free!" Tori reminded her. "Just ask God."

APPLICATION

When we want something so badly, we can miss the truth. The truth of God's word will set us free from the bondage we create trying to design our own truth. Reading God's word equals truth, but creating our own truth equals bondage. Reading God's word reveals His truth through the Holy Spirit! My sister, you can walk in truth.

PRAYER

Heavenly Father, I thank You for being the truth. I thank You that the Holy Spirit reveals the truth to me through Your word. Father, I thank You that the truth is available for me to freely. I desire to walk in truth by Your Grace and through the leading of the Holy Spirit. Father, I accept Your truth. In Jesus' name, I pray. Amen.

DAY 4
TEACHER

Are you a learner?

*"But the Comforter, which is the Holy Ghost,
whom the Father will send in my name, he shall
teach you all things and bring all things to your
remembrance, whatsoever I have said unto you."*
(JOHN 14:26)

STORY

Tori was feeling a bit overwhelmed. As she read her daily scripture, she heard the Spirit gently ask, "Are you a learner?" A light bulb turned on in her mind. Tori had not been a learner; she was only a reader. She had not allowed the Holy Spirit to teach her about what she read in God's word.

APPLICATION

In order to be learners, we must go deeper into the word of God and allow that word to rest in us and on us so the Holy Spirit can teach us the value of the word for the place we are in right now. Have you ever read a scripture at one time in your life, and it had no meaning? Then, a few months later or even a year later that same scripture arrested your attention when you read it. It became alive and real because you saw deeper into it; the Holy Spirit taught you at that moment how that scripture fit into your life. My dear sister, when you read God's word, let the Holy Spirit teach you!

PRAYER

Father God, in the matchless and amazing name of Jesus, I come to You, thanking You for Your word. Thank You, Father, for giving me Your word to comfort me and teach me! Help me, Father, to be a learner. In Jesus' name, Amen.

DAY 5
POWER

Are you using your superpowers?

"But ye shall receive power, after that the Holy Ghost is come upon you: and ye shall be witnesses unto me both in Jerusalem, and in all Judea, and in Samaria, and unto the uttermost part of the earth."

(ACTS 1:8)

STORY

Tori loved stories about superheroes. She often watched superhero movies, and even as a child, she watched the Saturday morning superhero cartoons. As she left church on Sunday, she could not get the sermon out of her head. The pastor preached about receiving God's power. As Tori thought about the message the rest of the day, she realized how she had always admired superheroes and how she had always wanted superpowers. Could she have superpowers?

Tori finally realized that day what she had missed her entire life. She had missed the fact that Jesus spoke superpowers into her life in the Bible! She was a superhero who had never used her superpowers. Tori had superpowers that love, forgive, comfort, and lead others to Christ. Once Tori finally realized that she had superpowers, she vowed to use them.

APPLICATION

Are you using your superpowers? If so, what are you using them to do? You can use your superpowers to tear down unjust systems and to help the poor. Are you using your superpowers to be a mentor or to love the unlovable? Are you using your superpowers to bring peace to a world of chaos? Your superpowers are within you. You may not have a magic lasso like Wonder Woman or x-ray vision like Superman, but you have the power of God that takes many forms. Do not let your superpowers go to waste. Use them for the glory of God.

PRAYER

Father God, in the name of Jesus, I thank You for Your word. Father, I thank You that You sent Your son Jesus and that He left me the Holy Spirit. I thank You that the Holy Spirit is my superpower! Father, I ask that I would be bold and use my superpowers to be a witness for You and draw people to the saving knowledge of Your son, Jesus Christ. In Jesus' name, I pray, Amen.

Bios

Stephanie Perry Moore – General Editor

Stephanie Perry Moore is the trailblazing author of the Payton Skky Series, the first African American, Christian teen series. She has written over sixty titles for children and adults. In addition to writing her own titles, she is the General Editor of several Bible products. Some of the releases include *Men of Color Study Bible, Wisdom and Grace Bible for Young Women of Color*, and the *Women of Color Devotional Bible*. Other titles that will be released this year are *Strength and Honor Bible for Young Men of Color, Women of Color Cookbook, Wisdom and Grace Devotional Bible*, and the *African-American Family Bible*. She is the Co-editor of REAL, an urban BibleZine published by Thomas Nelson and the Co-founder of the Sister's in Faith brand. She speaks in schools across the nation, uplifting youth. She lives in the greater Atlanta, Georgia area with her husband, Derrick Moore. They have three young adults. Visit her website at www. stephanieperrymoore.com

Jackie Graves Butts – Week 1 – Self-Care

Jackie Graves Butts is a Corporate Supply Chain Executive who loves to read and write in her spare time. She is a graduate of Auburn University where she received a BS degree in transportation and logistics. She is a covenant member of Word of Faith Family Cathedral in Austell, Georgia. Jackie loves to travel and dance like no one is looking. She knows that God's favor covers her as her shield, and because of this, she continues to live in the circle of His blessings, grace, and mercy. Jackie lives in the greater Atlanta area with her husband, Leonard, and their three children.

Dr. Charrita Danley Quimby – Week 2 – Creativity

Dr. Charrita Danley Quimby is an author, editor, publisher, and educator. Founder of Chideria Publishing, Inc., she provides writing, editing, and publishing services to a broad range of clients. Passionate about creating stories, Charrita is the author of the novel, *Through the Crack*, which chronicles a family's struggle to overcome drug addiction. She has written and edited numerous manuscripts, reports, grants, and other materials for individuals and organizations. In addition, she conducts presentations and workshops on various topics. Currently, Charrita serves as the Chief of Staff at Hampton University and Director of the Hampton University Press. A member of Delta Sigma Theta Sorority, Inc., she attended Tougaloo College, Louisiana State University, and Georgia State University, earning the BA, MA, and PhD degrees in English, respectively. A native of Mississippi, Charrita is married to Dr. Ronald Quimby, and their family includes one son and two daughters.

Orbra H. Porter – Week 3 – Father

Orbra H. Porter has a music ministry legacy at Cade Chapel M. B. Church where she has held significant roles such as Choir Director, Youth Church Director, and Sunday School Teacher. She has held positions as Communication Specialist with the General Missionary Baptist State Convention state music department and Secretary of the Music Auxiliary of their national Baptist affiliation. For more than 20 years, her music ministry has been enjoyed at local, state, regional, and national meetings of Delta Sigma Theta Sorority, Inc. of which she is a Golden Life member. Many have learned from Orbra's computer experience as a trainer and adjunct instructor. She enjoys singing with the Mississippi Mass Choir, and she has participated in many of their recordings over a span of over 30 years. Orbra lives in Jackson, Mississippi with Herman, her husband of 46 years. They are the parents of four adult children and have ten grandchildren.

Gwendolyn A. Mason – Week 4 – Fellowship

Gwendolyn A. Mason is the President/CEO of GABB Enterprise, a multi-dimensional communications company. She has spoken nationally and inspired many audiences to move to greater heights. Gwendolyn is also the Co-founder and Executive Director of the Stewart Foundation, a youth leadership development program targeting children between the ages of eight and eighteen. The foundation has impacted more than 20,000 youth over the course of its existence. It has made significant changes to youths' health and financial wellness, education, as well as their social and community involvement. She is a member of Delta Sigma Theta Sorority, Inc. where she committed herself to serving others as the National Arts and Letters Co-chair. She has served as the Executive Director for the "Walk Against the Call," breast cancer walk and has raised over $100,000 in monetary and in-kind donations. That walk is now called the "Pink Ribbon Walk." Gwendolyn is a native of Atlanta, Georgia, and the mother of three thriving young adults.

Sheryl Givens – Week 5 – Wisdom

Sheryl Givens was born and raised in Dayton, Ohio. She earned a BS degree in broadcast communication from Alabama State University and a MEd degree in early childhood education from Antioch McGregor University. She is a former kindergarten teacher and former assistant principal of a faith-based charter school. Mrs. Givens led a Christian academy as its director. After five years in that role, God called Sheryl to start her own enrichment program. She is also the Founder of GIRL TALK (God's Women Implementing Real Love), which is a women's empowerment group. She is a member of House of Hope, Atlanta, under the leadership of Pastor E. Dewey Smith. Sheryl lives in Conyers, Georgia with her husband, Rodney, and they have two children.

Jane Fox Long – Week 6 – Exploration

Jane Fox Long is the Director of Ministry Programming at Watts Chapel Missionary Baptist Church where she is also a member. She has been a member of Delta Sigma Theta Sorority, Inc. since 1982 and is an active member of the Raleigh Alumnae Chapter where she is a past president. Jane firmly believes that there is a place and purpose for everyone. She is grateful for the opportunity to pour into God's people and prays that something she says or does will touch the heart of the receiver. She is a native of New Jersey and navigated to North Carolina where she currently resides with her husband, Craig. She has three children and eight grandloves.

First Lady Wayneshia Harris Perrymond – Week 7 – Patience

First Lady Wayneshia Harris Perrymond is a devout Christian woman of God. She lives in McDonough, Georgia with her husband, Roderick Perrymond, who is the Pastor of New Love Tabernacle Christian Church. They have two children, Autumn and Roderick "RJ." Wayneshia attended Georgia Southern University where she earned a bachelor's degree. Later, she earned a master's degree from Fort Valley State University. On December 14, 2019, she graduated from the University of West Alabama with her specialist degree in school counseling. She enjoys working with middle school children and has been working patiently with them for the past nineteen years. She also enjoys working with the youth ministry at her church. It brings her heart joy to see the youth blossom into young Christian men and women. She is grateful to have the opportunity to write for the Lord.

Michele Clark Jenkins – Week 8 – Integrity

Michele Clark Jenkins, Co-founder of the Sisters in Faith brand, published by Thomas Nelson Publishers is the author and editor of *She Speaks* (Thomas Nelson), Co-editor and contributing writer to *The Sisters in Faith Bible* (Thomas Nelson) and *Real: The Complete New Testament Biblezine* (Thomas Nelson). She is also a contributing writer and editor of the *Children of Color Storybook Bible* (Thomas Nelson) contributing writer for the *Women of Color Devotional Bible* (Nia Publishing/World), and the *Wisdom and Grace Devotional Bible* (Nia Publishing/World). Michele and her husband, Kym, are elders at Liberty Church, Marietta, Georgia and have three daughters. Please visit her at facebook.com/thesistersinfaith

Tia McCollors – Week 9 – Doer

Tia McCollors is a bestselling author, speaker, and writing coach. Her first Christian novel *A Heart of Devotion* was an Essence Magazine bestseller. Other bestselling titles followed, including *Zora's Cry, The Last Woman Standing,* and *Steppin' Into the Good Life.* Her *Days of Grace* series (*Friday Night Love, Sunday Morning Song,* and *Monday Morning*

Joy) continues to grow in popularity. In addition to ten novels, Tia has penned several nonfiction projects, including a devotion titled, *If These Shoes Could Talk*. When she is not writing, she finds passion in delivering inspiring and faith-based messages to women about how to maximize their lives. She is a member of Alpha Kappa Alpha Sorority, Inc. Her enthusiastic messages encourage women to embrace their true calling, journey through life with purpose, and cultivate the confidence and dedication to meet their goals. Tia and her husband, Wayne, live with their three children in the greater Atlanta area.

Dr. Lakeba Hibbler Williams – Week 10 – Perseverance

Dr. Lakeba Hibbler Williams is a Licensed Professional Counselor (LPC) and a National Certified Counselor (NCC) with a BS in social work from Southern University A&M College in Baton Rouge, LA, an MEd in community agency counseling, and a PhD in adult education, both from Auburn University in Auburn, AL. She has extensive training in counseling clients suffering from the devastating effects of childhood abuse and trauma. Her mission is to teach clients healthier, more effective ways to cope with depression, anxiety, family conflict, relationship issues, and grief. She is the Owner/ Director of Fresh Hope Counseling Center, LLC. She also works part-time with the City of Atlanta's Psychological Services/Employee Assistance Program as a Behavioral Health Specialist. An author, educator, and consultant with over 25 years of experience, she is passionate about psychoeducation as well as mental health and wellness. She also serves as a speaker and workshop leader at global, national, and regional events for universities, churches, and corporations on a variety of topics, including mental health and wellness, healthy relationships, and leadership. An active volunteer in her community, she lives in Decatur, Georgia with her family.

Dr. Rindia Lambert Hunt – Week 11 – Thriving

Dr. Rindia Lambert Hunt is a native of Huntsville, Alabama. She is an educator at Tuskegee University where she serves as Assistant Professor and Academic Fieldwork Coordinator for the Occupational Therapy Program. She serves as a Deaconess, Vacation Bible School Director, Willing Working member and Youth Leader at White Street Baptist Church in Auburn, Alabama. In addition, she serves as President of the Exceptional Outreach Organization Board, which is a nonprofit organization serving individuals with disabilities in Lee County. She serves as Co-advisor for the Delta Gems Program and an active member of the Auburn Alumnae Chapter of Delta Sigma Theta Sorority, Inc. She is a graduate, cum laude, from Alabama A&M University where she received a BS degree in medical technology with a minor in chemistry. She holds a MS degree in occupational therapy and doctorate in occupational therapy from Belmont University in Nashville, Tennessee. Dr. Rindia Lambert Hunt lives in Auburn, Alabama with her husband, Mr. Rogers Hunt, and their two teenage sons.

Kymberlee Norsworthy – Week 12 – Armor

Kymberlee Norsworthy is a seasoned public relations strategist and published writer.

With a professional background that includes Chief of Publicity for RCA Inspiration/ Sony Music, as well as senior positions at Rogers & Cowan and Interscope Records, Kymberlee has helped develop, protect, and promote personalities and brands for more than 20 years. She has focused on elevating faith-based brands since 2006, creating opportunities with BET, *Late Night with Jimmy Fallon*, *Good Morning America*, *The New York Times*, and more. Kymberlee has written for *Rolling Out Newsweekly* and ESPN's *The Undefeated*, in both instances lending a faith-based perspective to these mainstream media outlets. She also founded the website *This Gospel Life*, which highlights and celebrates the dynamic lifestyle of faith. Kymberlee lives in Jersey City, New Jersey with her ASPCA-adopted cat.

First Lady Jamell Meeks – Week 13 – Holy Spirit

First Lady Jamell Meeks is the Director of Women's Ministries for the Salem Baptist Church of Chicago, under the leadership of her husband, Reverend James T. Meeks. Women of Influence serves over 4,000 women. She serves as National Chair for First Ladies Health Initiative and leader of a national pastors' wives prayer group. First Lady Meeks has been featured in several national publications for her work with entrepreneurship, women, and health. She is a certified John Maxwell speaker and speaks to hundreds of women annually. She developed the nationally recognized A.R.I.S.E Entrepreneur Program in 2004. The program has helped over 1,100 people start and grow their small businesses. Her mission is to inspire women of all ages to live a life grounded by faith, guided by purpose, and motivated by infinite possibilities. She resides in Chicago, Illinois with her husband. She is the mother of four children and a proud grandmother of four.

GOALS

Become an US Urban Spirit! Publishing and Media Company
Independent or Church Distributor Today!

- earn extra money
- engage with more people
- change lives
- join a winning team
- distribute high-quality Bibles and books

Go to www.urbanspirit.biz

Order your Independent or Church Distributor
"Starter Kit" today online. It contains everything you need
to get started selling right away.
Or call **800.560.1690** to get started today!

WOMEN COLOR
DAILY DEVOTIONAL

Winter
EDITION

$14.99
ISBN 978-0-9884572-2-5

51499>

9 780988 457225

LARGE PRINT

WOMEN of COLOR
DAILY DEVOTIONAL

Spring
EDITION

$14.99
ISBN 978-0-9846480-9-2
51499>

9 780984 648092

LARGE PRINT

WOMEN COLOR

DAILY DEVOTIONAL

Summer
EDITION

$14.99
ISBN 978-0-9881958-2-0
51499>

9 780988 195820

WOMEN COLOR

DAILY DEVOTIONAL

Fall
EDITION

$14.99
ISBN 978-0-9884572-6-3
51499>

9 780988 457263